THE BLISS
CODES

You deserve to be healed

NATALIE RESTREPO

TABLE OF CONTENTS

About the Author

Natalie Restrepo is the proud owner of *House of Vibration*, where she masterfully integrates ancient wisdom with modern-day healing, transforming the coaching and business world. As an energetic business consultant, Natalie is on a mission to remind high-achievers that they can thrive as corporate powerhouses while maintaining their spiritual hygiene and living in divine alignment.

For the first decade of her career, Natalie seemed to have it all. As a top executive for one of the world's biggest celebrity business moguls, she generated over $50 million in revenue, trained top producers, and built a flashy, high-powered lifestyle. Her title impressed everyone—but deep inside, she felt unfulfilled. She craved more than sales numbers and accolades; she longed for meaningful conversations and knew the world didn't need more closers—it needed healing.

Caught in the whirlwind of corporate success, Natalie felt torn. She knew her true gifts were meant for a higher purpose, but the fear of losing everything she had worked for kept her stuck. Finally, she chose to risk it all for a soul-centered mission: creating *House of Vibration*. What began in a humble studio has blossomed into a thriving community brand, a space where business and spirituality coexist.

Today, Natalie empowers others to awaken their innate gifts and move beyond merely visualizing their dreams—she helps them bring those dreams to life in the physical world. Through energy work, coaching, and actionable strategies, she guides her clients toward their highest potential.

At *House of Vibration*, Natalie and her team provide personalized support to help clients connect with their true purpose and create a life that aligns with their deepest values. Her journey is proof that it's possible to succeed in business while staying deeply rooted in your spiritual essence.

THE BLISS
CODES

The Bliss Codes challenges you to view your life as a sacred text, wherein lies the instructions for unlocking the deepest layers of spiritual wisdom. It speaks to the heart of those who yearn for a deeper connection with the divine, offering guidance on how to navigate the complexities of life with courage and purpose. This book is a celebration of the power of faith, the resilience of the human spirit, and the boundless possibilities that lie within the realm of spiritual exploration.

At the heart of this guide is the understanding that every challenge we face is an invitation to expand our consciousness, to grow, and to evolve. "Embracing the Infinite" offers practical tools and insights for transforming life's difficulties into stepping stones, encouraging readers to approach problems with a mindset of opportunity. It gently guides you through a process of rebirthing, where you emerge with a new vision of the world—a vision marked by a deeper understanding of your purpose and a renewed sense of purpose and direction.

"The Bliss Codes" teaches you how to translate this consciousness into actionable steps that can be implemented in your daily life.

Let this book guide you as you peel back the layers of your being, uncover the eight divine codes within, and activate them to create the highest timeline for yourself and embody the version of you aligned with your sacred path.

About the Book

A book written for all of the healers, leaders, teachers, artists, poets, protectors, and prophets of the world.For all those who feel called to serve, create, and lead with their whole hearts for the greater good of all mankind.

The Bliss Codes is your invitation to activate the divine blueprint within and live in love with your most profound mission. This book acknowledges the deep yearning within those called to make a difference, offering guidance to unlock the latent power and purpose that resides in each of us. We are intricately designed by our creator with many codes, complete as a whole, perfect in every aspect. By learning how to activate eight of these codes we can be led to experience profound bliss. The journey to unlocking this bliss lies in learning how to activate these codes through consciousness.

Natalie Restrepo, author of The Bliss Codes is a modern-day healer, coach, and energetic business consultant who walks you through her journey from early encounters with the supernatural to navigating the challenges of adolescence and the vicious world of corporate America. Natalie's story is a testament to the power of inner work and the transformative potential of embracing our true selves.

With each word as a reminder that you are never truly alone, a profound compassion and clarity through the discovery of eight sacred codes—keys to unlocking the deepest bliss within ourselves.

The Bliss Codes challenges you to view your life as a sacred text, wherein lies the instructions for unlocking the deepest layers of spiritual wisdom. It speaks to the heart of those who seek a deeper connection with the divine.

You can embrace "The Bliss Codes" in its entirety or in times of confusion or seeking immediate insight, simply open the book to any page—let the code you land on serve as a beacon, illuminating the path forward and offering a clearer understanding of life's lessons. Each code, each page, is a mirror reflecting the truth of our existence and the lessons we are meant to learn, perfectly timed to the moment of our questioning.

By using "The Bliss Codes" in this manner, you engage in a sacred dialogue with the universe, allowing the synchronicity of your spirit and the divine guidance of the book to lead you toward enlightenment. Whether you seek comprehensive transformation or immediate understanding, this book is a powerful ally, ready to reveal the depths of wisdom already present in your life's journey.

At the heart of this guide is the understanding that every challenge we face is an invitation to expand our consciousness, grow, and evolve. "Embracing the Infinite" offers practical tools and insights for transforming life's difficulties into stepping stones, encouraging readers to approach problems with a mindset of opportunity.

Bliss Code Foreword

It is a profound time to be alive. As the Galactic Seasons shift and we align with the Great Central Sun, we are being activated by the solar flares and encouraged by the universal alignment of the spheres to remember, activate and embody our Divine Human Nature.

Mother Earth intends to evolve into higher consciousness at this time in accordance with the natural galactic seasons. We can either surrender to this energy and accompany Mother Earth in her ascension to a higher timeline or we can resist and fall back into yet another cycle of learning through karmic cycles. The choice is ours according to our own Free Will.

We are awakening and walking each other home. Finally reuniting with our soul tribes and witnessing the interwoven nature of our individual purposes acknowledging that in truth, they are One. To be in love with being alive… to be in love with being Life… to be Love, to be Life! Honoring our unity by making our diversity sacred.

Encoded in your DNA there are dormant Bliss Codes. This book acts as a key, the words herein activating your genetic blueprint and giving you greater access to your Highest Self who can see across all time and space with the aid of your genetic ancestral disposition. This is your birth right. To be at home within the body. To be a bridge from heaven to earth. To experience nothing and everything. To experience mortality and immortality. To express and share what you find by exploring the inner and outer landscapes. You are a pillar of light. A rainbow bridge. The ancient wisdom lives within you and it is safe to share this now. These are prophetic times. We are ancient beings who have returned to activate and embody bliss on this planet.

I am so grateful to Natalie for sharing her story, In sharing her story and discovery Natalie shines a light with her wisdom that uncovers the wisdom within us all and the bliss that is ours to clain. This book aims to unlock these sacred codes within your soul in a way that can be easily accessed, explored and practiced to aid in our journey of self-discovery, alchemy, reclamation and embodiment. In these pages you may find the answer to questions you didn't even know you were asking. This is the power of authenticity and bliss shared. This is the power of expressing the truth of our human experience. Like mirrors reflecting light, like a match in the darkness, together we illuminate the way home to the moment that is now.

"May you find what your soul seeks in these pages.
May these words be a key to a deeper part of you.
May this book be a talisman of protection and medicine for
your soul.

May you be led towards your highest bliss.
May you find solace and comfort in knowing that you never
walk alone.

Aloha Ma, Self-reflective love
In Lak'ech Ala K'in, I am another you as you are another me
Ubuntu, I am because we are
Aho, Mitakuye Oyasin, All My Relations."

MAHINA ALEXANDER

To all of my brothers and sisters doing the inner work

Our great spirit assigned a specific role to you, he reminds us everyday that he made you perfect in every single way as he makes no mistakes. Creator has given us many inner sacred codes, eight of which I have discovered to be keys to unlocking the deepest bliss within ourselves. These codes are ancient wisdoms, embedded in our souls, waiting patiently for us to awaken them.

In this guide my goal is to help you find conscious enlightenment and activate them. You are not broken and you are not meant to live a life full of suffering. These codes will release any burdonsen that any man has pushed upon themselves..

The eight Bliss codes are our medicine allowing us to walk in the beauty and abundance of our temporary home a sweet taste of heaven on Earth as intended. Together we will heal the wounds instead of spreading the pain because that is true strength.

Once these eight codes have been activated you will come to understand why you were sent here to share this experience with me.

I extend my gratitude to you for embarking on this sacred journey, investing your time and energy in aligning with a deeper, more ancient part of yourself. Please approach this path with grace, patience and perseverance, for the Great Spirit will guide our steps, as we take into our hands the healing and transformation we seek. This book is for all those who are making their way home, those who serve, and those who nurture the creatures of this Earth. Thank you for all that you do for this planet.

Part One | Origin Story

The 8th Sense

In our early days, most of our mothers, whether consciously or not, create a shielding barrier around us with their powerful prayers of protection from the moment we enter their wombs. These powerful blessings create energetic bubbles around us to help us get through our scariest nightmares and reroute us back to the comfort of our mother's arms.

My first memories are just that. I can literally see the pastel pinks of my crib and hear the 1992 top hit "Just Another Day" by Jon Secada playing from my father's radio. No one believes me, but I remember these exact moments. My mother can confirm she would play that song over and over. It's still a banger in my book!

As I grew older, I depended more and more on my parents' prayers, I was constantly terrified by seeing things no one else seemed to be able to see. I would wake up in the middle of the night to whispers, little fairy-looking figures, human-shaped spectres, and shadow people. Most children experience these supernatural encounters; it's actually supernatural. "Out of the mouth of babes and sucklings hast thou ordained strength." This means that children, in their innocence and simplicity, often speak profound truths or wisdom that adults might overlook or fail to recognise.

As I grew, I needed those prayers even more, especially when I started seeing and hearing things others didn't. I learned that I had a special gift; I could connect with spirits. Learning and unlearning became my journey. I found out I was a medium, someone who can communicate with the other side.

School wasn't easy for me. I stumbled along the way, even failing fourth grade. It was during these struggles that I was diagnosed with dyslexia, which made learning and reading a tough mountain to climb. On top of that, my encounters with the supernatural world didn't make things any easier. They set me apart, making my path through school even more challenging. My mother stood by me and did what any Hispanic mother would do: she worked the system and somehow got me a scholarship at a private school.

She believed that a different environment would make a difference, one that could offer me the support and understanding I needed. It was a small Catholic school run by a community of Haitians in Miami. I learned a lot there. My childhood was full of learning, exploring, and sometimes rebelling.

I got through my childhood as a sweet, funny little flower. I broke out into my teen years to be a radically wild teenager who dabbled in quite a bit of psychedelic drugs and placed myself in a few terrifying situations.

As my ability to connect with the unseen world grew, so did the guidance from my spiritual mentors, urging me to deepen my bond with the Creator. This guidance was like a compass, steering me through life's storms with grace. It's this grace that whispered paths of safety, pulling me back just before I could tumble into trouble. This protective veil didn't just guard my spirit; it sculpted my destiny, leading me through the maze of life to moments of unexpected triumph.

Guided With Grace

I always seemed to save myself from bad situations before they became really BAD! Graduating high school, navigating college, and landing a dream job by 22—a feat that seemed like a miracle—was a testament to my mother's prayers being answered. But it wasn't just luck. It was the power of understanding deeper truths—the power of agreement with the universe and the vibrant soul of money—that propelled me forward. While others lost themselves to fleeting pleasures, I dedicated myself to mastering my craft, becoming a conduit for success in a world obsessed with the bottom line.

I devoted myself to my career as a master closer. This dream job included someone very particular, a billionaire sales trainer who happened to take a liking to me and taught me all of his ways. Maybe he saw something special in me, or maybe I was just in the right place at the right time. Either way, I am eternally grateful no matter the controversy his name carries. I learned how to manage large numbers of people, turn bad situations into profitable outcomes, and met some of the most extraordinary individuals that I carry in my heart forever.

In this space, I helped many businesses and individuals who were, more often than not, at their lowest point. I was constantly faced with the realization that I needed to question my own outlook on money, spirituality, and integrity. It challenged my perceptions of wealth, spiritual depth, and ethical living.

Why do we burden ourselves with such gravity, I wondered, when the essence of life flows so freely around us? Why does life seem to carry such a weight of seriousness for everyone? I was sure it was not meant to be lived so heavily.

My job was HARDCORE! In the beginning, I hated being around such narcissistic, money-hungry, greedy individuals. The thought of enduring this atmosphere for more than six months seemed daunting; I couldn't imagine lasting a day longer. Those six months turned into eight years of absolute and unwavering commitment.

What I enjoyed the most wasn't bringing in over $50 million in revenue but developing and training my team. As I took on this journey of helping these beams of light, I took on the responsibility of developing myself and becoming the most enlightened version of myself I could possibly be. These eight years were a testament not to my tolerance for the environment, but to my transformation within.

This commitment to growth led me down a path of relentless search for answers. I delved into the realms of philosophy, spirituality, and human psychology, seeking wisdom that could expand my consciousness. As I grew, so did my ability to influence and inspire those around me. I aimed to create a space where the pursuit of financial success was balanced with ethical conduct and personal growth. This meant challenging the prevailing norms of our industry, advocating for a culture where success was measured not just by revenue but by the impact we had on each other's lives and the world at large.

Navigating the corporate maze with a vibe that totally clashed with the old-school suit-and-tie scene, I managed to climb to the top as an executive in the company, rocking my leather boots the whole way. Despite the side-eyes for my teaching style, view on life, inked skin, and ditching the expected blazer for boots look, I proved all the doubters wrong. My rise challenged the stereotypical image of leadership. By embracing my true self and valuing diverse perspectives, I fostered a culture of innovation and inclusivity.

As I climbed the career ladder and took on the role of provider for my family, a part of me felt like I was drifting from what truly made me special. Amidst the success, my passion for human rights and my connection to both the spiritual and physical worlds started to feel neglected. This realisation hit me hard—I was more than my job title and the financial support I offered my family. My soul was craving the fulfilment of my deeper dreams and values.

Acknowledging this disconnect, I embarked on a quest to realign my professional path with my personal convictions. I knew I had to find a way to integrate my activism and spiritual journey into my career. This wasn't about choosing one over the other but about merging my passion with my profession to create a truly fulfilling life.

This journey reminded me that true success is about more than financial achievements; it's about making a difference and staying true to oneself. I began to search for answers, diving deeper into my purpose and the impact I wanted to have on the world.

Angels all around us

Amidst this journey of finding balance and reigniting my passion, I felt a strong desire to connect with my guardian angels. As soon as I made that decision, one unexpected night, I woke up to a mesmerising sphere of light right before my eyes, a perfect orb of laser-like brilliance that left me in awe. This extraordinary sight sparked an insatiable curiosity in me to discover its origin and meaning.

Soon after, a serendipitous moment came through a Facebook ad for a psychic fair at a metaphysical church in West Palm Beach, Florida. Feeling drawn to this, I convinced a friend to join me, stepping into the unknown with an open heart, unaware of how pivotal this decision would be for my journey and the book I was destined to write.

Upon arrival, the place was unlike anything I expected, reminiscent of a Catholic church but with an eclectic, almost whimsical vibe that could easily be dismissed by sceptics. Despite my initial reservations, I was there for answers. I chose a tarot angel card reader, hoping for some clarity but not expecting the profound impact it would have.

I kept my question to myself as to what this encounter with the sphere was and went ahead with the session. The reading introduced me to Archangel Metatron, the angel associated with sacred geometry and seen as a bridge between the divine (Source energy or God) and those of us seeking a deeper spiritual connection. This concept of THE BRIDGE resonated with me on a profound level.

Archangel Metatron became a pivotal moment, serving as a bridge between the divine and my human experiences. His ties to sacred geometry and the Akashic Records perfectly matched my quest for deeper spiritual insights. When I witnessed a mysterious sphere of light, it was more than just a sign; it was a direct call to explore beyond the surface of my existence. Metatron's presence in my life symbolised my awakening to a higher calling. It made me realize that angels and spiritual guides are constantly around us, offering direction and insights through subtle signs and messages. This encounter encouraged me to pay closer attention to the guidance offered by beings like Metatron, who watch over our spiritual paths.

Metatron is often depicted holding a cube, known as Metatron's Cube, which is a symbol of sacred geometry containing all the geometric shapes in God's creation and representing the patterns that make up everything the universe holds. This cube is said to be a tool that Metatron uses to clear away lower energies and align your vibrational energies with peace and balance. In spiritual practices, Archangel Metatron is called upon for guidance related to spiritual development, learning, and understanding the mysteries of the universe. He also assists those who are sensitive, particularly children and adults who are often referred to as Indigos or Crystals, helping them to harness their sensitivities as gifts.

From that moment, my mission crystallized. I launched House of Vibration, hosting retreats, workshops, training, reiki sessions, sound healing, and other healing services as well as energetic consulting. I was not only to cross this bridge myself but also to guide others across it, facilitating their journey towards spiritual enlightenment and understanding. This book is the story of my journey and is dedicated to that mission. It's about sharing the insights, experiences, and connections I've made with the spiritual realm, offering a pathway for others to explore their own connections with the divine.

Throughout my path to sculpting the life I dreamed of, I discovered that it's indeed possible to have it all—to experience heaven on earth and find bliss within.

Now, when I mention this, it's essential to grasp the gravity of the statement. Achieving this state is not without its sacrifices; it's intense, often painful, and demands a great deal from us but never suffering. Yet, it's within our power to decide whether to endure a life marked by suffering or to embrace one free from fear, illness, loneliness, and pain. This blissful existence is what we yearn for most during our time on earth, and deep down, we all know that we have a specific purpose to fulfil in our human experience even if we can't seem to remember it.

My curiosity led me to explore why some seem to have it all figured out while others struggle. My connection to the creative spirit revealed numerous miracles, propelling me to delve into ancient wisdom and the foundational texts that have guided civilizations. The lessons were surprisingly simple—for instance, the Bible teaches that Jesus's sacrifice was meant to spare us from a life of suffering, Buddishisum speaks about Nirvana, Hinduism suggests that suffering results from ignorance, Judaism teaches that humans have free will and are responsible for their choices. While suffering can result from poor choices, all the codes you need are already within you, waiting to be activated.

Inspired by the seven chakras and life itself, I've crafted a step-by-step guide to reassure you that you're not alone or flawed. This guide centers on the idea that every challenge is an opportunity for growth and expansion. "Embracing the Infinite" provides practical tools and insights to turn life's obstacles into opportunities, fostering a mindset geared towards seeing problems as chances for growth.

It walks you through a rebirthing process, at the end of which you'll view the world with new eyes, enriched by a profound comprehension of your purpose, imbued with a rejuvenated sense of direction and purpose.

Deeply rooted in the essence of who we are and the lineage from which we come. It's an exploration that requires us to delve into the very foundation of our existence, acknowledging and taking responsibility for not only our past but the past of our ancestors as well. This process, known as ancestral healing, recognizes that the lives and experiences of our forebears significantly influence our present and future.

"Unlearning is as sacred as learning"

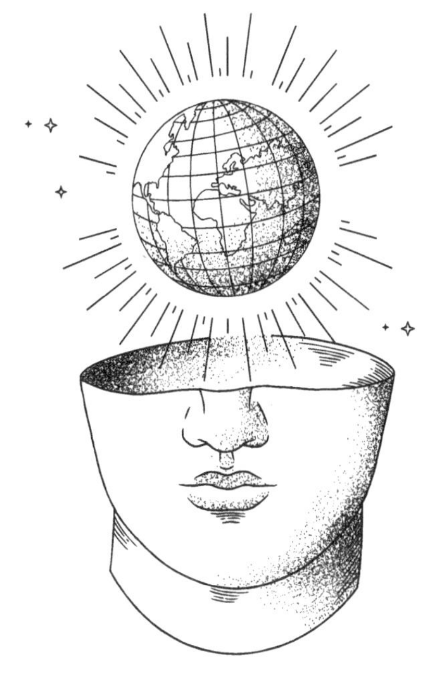

CODE ONE

-Rooted with Ancestral Inheritance-

Only look back to see how far you've come.
Embracing ancestral heritage and healing
becomes the bridge to healing from our roots
inviting us to take ownership of our spiritual and
emotional legacy, and in doing so, nurturing
the strength to flourish in the present grounded
in the wisdom of our ancestors.

Bliss is Your Birthright

As you begin to integrate these codes into your healing journey, let me remind you that it might sometimes look different than media portrays it to be. During this process, you will slowly or rapidly feel an awakening, bringing shifts to your perspective and new aspects of yourself and your wounding to light. You may revisit old and familiar patterns through a different lens with these tools. Often, this journey leads us to shadows of ourselves that make us feel far from a goddess or a warrior and more like a hermit. This is a natural part of the inward call.

As we uncover stories from our family or past stored in the vault of secrets through narratives we have created or inherited, we are often faced with the discomfort inherent in the reality shifts brought on by an awakening. When the third eye starts to open, we begin to see those things that we have been afraid to face, like a glimmer lifting. This journey often demands courage from us; you can only ascend as deep as you are rooted. So let's ground into our path as we walk this process together.

Healing starts with the root—the base of our being, our connection to the earth, and our ancestry. It's about understanding that it's not just the genetic traits of our ancestors that we carry with us but their emotional and spiritual legacies as well. This includes the traumas, patterns, and unresolved issues that have been passed down through generations.

By confronting these ancestral wounds, we start to untangle the influences that have unconsciously guided our choices, behaviors, and beliefs. Taking responsibility for our past involves a deep, often challenging examination of the ways in which our lineage has shaped us. It requires a willingness to face the discomfort and pain that might arise as we uncover the truths of our family's history. But it's through this process that we start to release the burdens we've been carrying—burdens that may not have originated with us but have influenced us nonetheless. It's about learning that they aren't even burdens, simply lessons that must be learned during this experience.

Ancestral healing is about breaking cycles that no longer serve us, freeing ourselves and future generations from repeating patterns of suffering. It's a path of transformation that allows us to heal not only our wounds but those of our ancestors as well, creating a ripple effect of healing across time. This journey of healing from the ground up is a powerful act of reclaiming our wholeness, acknowledging that we are the sum of many generations before us. It's an invitation to forge a new path—one that honors our past, heals our present, and shapes a future filled with greater awareness, understanding, and peace. As we embark on this process, we reconnect with our roots in a way that nurtures our growth, grounding us firmly in the knowledge of who we are and where we come from, and empowering us to move forward with grace and resilience.

"You are the new ancestor; act accordingly."

It's deeper than the skin; understanding that we are not merely individuals navigating through life but are deeply interconnected with our lineage is a profound realization. This connection is not just about the physical resemblance we bear to our parents but extends to the very essence of who we are, our skin—the laughter we share, the shape of our toes, and even the way we view the world. These traits, inherited through generations, serve as a testament to the complex web of life that we are part of.

From countless threads made of memories, experiences, and stories passed down through our DNA, these inherited memories act as armor, equipping us to face life's myriad challenges. They are not merely remnants of the past but living, breathing aspects of our being, influencing how we navigate our present and shape our future. Understanding the depth of our lineage involves recognizing that we carry within us a vast library of information. This library is replete with traditions, stories, and wisdom accumulated over generations. It's a memory vault that, while invisible to the naked eye, profoundly impacts our lives.

For example, growing up, you might have heard family members tell you as a child how much you resemble your parents' features. Sometimes these features are even deeper than skin. I personally carry my mother's laughter and my father's ugly toes. All of this is memory, karmic inherited memory that passed down to us to shield us through our battles. We are a tapestry of information, full of inherited traditions and stories. A memory vault that is bestowed upon us through our DNA.

At a simple glance, you may think about your mother and father as a union, and through that union, you came to be; however, this perspective barely scratches the surface of our true heritage. We are extensions of a long line of ancestors, each contributing to the mosaic of our identity. Our beliefs, viewpoints, and even the traumas we bear are not solely our own but are inherited from those who came before us. You are not just a result of a consummation; you are an extension of them. I like to think that most of the things we carry are all of their beautiful qualities, but that is not always the case. As we carry forward their dharma, we may also carry forward their karma. This is our foundation. It's the root from which true health, well-being, and empowerment grow. It's the core on which our physical and energetic body is built. These elements form the foundation of our being, influencing our health, well-being, and sense of empowerment. They are rooted deep within us, shaping both our physical and energetic bodies. This ancestral memory vault, associated with the lower spine, serves as a reminder of our connection to our lineage and the collective human experience.

By turning our gaze inward and exploring the depths of our inherited memories, we can begin to understand ourselves in relation to the continuum of human existence. This introspection allows us to appreciate the beauty of our inheritance while also confronting and healing the inherited traumas. In doing so, we honor our ancestors and embrace the fullness of our potential, grounded in the rich soil of our shared human heritage.

As you embark on this awakening journey, pause to reflect on where you stand right now. You may feel the call to help humanity, sensing signs and wonders unfolding around you. But before turning to the vast insights of the third eye, remember to root yourself deeply in the wisdom of your foundation. This journey calls for vision, yes, but vision anchored by the strength of your roots, honoring where you have come from so that you may rise purposefully.

Start at the beginning; honor each step. The roots sustain us, grounding our understanding of the past as we are guided by what is yet to come. This sacred balance lets us move forward without losing sight of what supports us—step by step, we awaken, not just to the world but to the journey that has prepared us to transform it.

Be the Break in the Chain of Patrimonial Suffering

In life, you might have faced situations where you felt that you had tried everything in your power to win a certain battle. These battles can be seen in our personal relationships, both romantic and business, as well as in health, career, or even within our own relationships with ourselves.

This then poses questions like, "What's wrong with me?" "Why is this happening to me?" "I have done all I can to be better." Not feeling comfortable in our own skin. Being faced with a constant feeling of void and emptiness. This homesick feeling is deeply burning and painful, causing anxiety, and depression, and can sometimes be replaced by an unhealthy ego of greed and lack of true purpose.

I am here to tell you that you are not alone. We are linked, and in order for me to live a blissful life, I must share these instruments with you. In order for me to win, you must win with me! Take shelter, and let's walk home. Listen to me when I tell you that the battle is just a dance between the physical and spiritual. While what you are experiencing may not necessarily be your fault, in order for you to advance, you must take ownership of all of you. The only way we can make changes is by taking the wheel. You will not be chosen to be the light of your family or to be a successful doctor or a famous singer. You will have to make the decision to do so. Choose yourself and take the wheel. Start saying, "It is all mine, and I take full-hearted responsibility." Many of us choose to carry baggage. Some of this weight has come from events like oppression, trauma, slavery, emigration, or genocide—heavy stories your forebears carried. Ancestral healing becomes a cure for situations like these, reverse engineering—a backward healing process that ripples through timelines. The most beautiful part of this is that when you make the decision to take full responsibility for your history, you are not only healing yourself but also curing the future of our generations, those who will come after you. It's not just merely about the generations to come, your children and grandchildren, but also the enduring harmony of our cosmos.

Even if you think, "I don't intend to have children," remember that being woven into the fabric of our earthly existence means we are intrinsically connected with our planet, leaving our mark irrespective of lineage. In the embrace of the sun, our father, and

the earth, our mother, we are all a piece of the human collective
and get to make empowered choices about what we want to bring
forward and pass on to the generations to come after us.

Those who came before us are deeply intertwined with
your essence, and establishing a connection with them opens
pathways to revisit and resolve unfinished journeys. Through
this bond, their achievements and endeavors find resolution and
fulfillment in and through you. If we can inherit trauma, then surely
we must also inherit blessings.

The Key Principles of Ancestral Healing

It starts with you. Initiate the journey with self-healing, striving
earnestly towards profound awareness. To decipher the messages
from your forebears accurately, your mind must be a sanctuary,
unclouded, inviting visions with clarity. Reading this book and
doing the work is one step forward on your sacred path. Like the
clear waters of a mountain spring, your mind must be pure and
receptive, ready to catch the reflections of ancestral wisdom.

Meet your Ancestors. Embrace your lineage and recognize
their unwavering support. Visualize your ancestral guides as your
spiritual squad, a dedicated ensemble of encouragers, uniquely
yours. Some guides walk beside you in this realm, safeguarding
your journey; these may manifest as family, companions, or
even animals. Others exist in a celestial realm, like angels and
saints, ethereal entities guiding you from afar, achieving their
transcendence and fulfilling their existential purpose through your
actions. Heed their silent prayers for you. Notice their signals
in the mundane and the magical—pennies, feathers, melodies,
butterflies, ladybugs, or moments of serenity and elation, even in
the subtle ringing in your ears. In these signs, feel the presence
of your ancestors, as constant and enduring as the sun and the
stars.

Break toxic patterns. Dismantle harmful legacies. Reflect
on behaviors ingrained in you, passed forward through your
lineage. Consider beliefs and opinions embedded deep within as
fundamental truths. What are some habits that you naturally do
that have been passed down from your parents? For example,
political or religious viewpoints that have been instilled as core
beliefs. By recognizing and understanding these patterns, you
honor the wisdom of your ancestors while also freeing yourself

from the chains of outdated beliefs, stepping into a future of your own making. Like the eagle soaring high above, gain a broader perspective on your life and choices, breaking free from the constraints of the past.

Embrace this sacred journey with the spirit of a warrior and the heart of a healer, knowing you are guided and supported by those who came before you. As you walk this path, blend the ancient wisdom with your modern experience, creating a harmonious dance between the old and the new. In the quiet moments, listen to the whispers of your ancestors, and in the busy moments, feel their strength lifting you. This journey of ancestral healing is not just about looking back but also about moving forward with a deeper understanding of who you are and where you come from, carrying the light of your heritage into the future.

WALK LIKE YOU HAVE 10,000 ANCESTORS WALKING BEHIND YOU.

Healing Prompts Exercise

This exercise is a heartfelt journey into the core of your ancestral beliefs, offering a path to understand the values passed down through your lineage. It aims to illuminate which beliefs serve your highest good and which may be ready to be lovingly released as part of your ancestral healing journey.

Step 1: Identify Shared Convictions

1. **Reflect on Your Beliefs:** Sit in a quiet space and contemplate your core beliefs and convictions. These are the guiding stars of your life, the principles that shape your actions and decisions.

2. **Consider Your Parents' Beliefs:** With a compassionate heart, think about the beliefs and values your parents hold dear. These might be explicitly stated or subtly demonstrated through their actions.

3. **List Three Shared Convictions:** Write down three beliefs or convictions that you and your parents both cherish. These could span from spiritual values to attitudes about education, work, or relationships.

Example:

- You and your parents both hold the belief in the transformative power of hard work.

- You and your parents both value honesty and integrity in all relationships.

- You and your parents both prioritize the importance of family gatherings and maintaining close family ties.

Step 2: Identify Differing Beliefs

1. **Reflect on Diverging Views:** With an open mind, consider the areas where your beliefs diverge from those of your parents. These differences might have been points of contention or simply reflections of evolving perspectives.

2. **List Three Differing Beliefs:** List three beliefs or convictions where you and your parents differ. For each belief, also ponder whether these differences might be rooted in the beliefs held by their parents (your grandparents).

Example:

- You embrace a more flexible parenting style, while your parents were strict disciplinarians.

- You explore various spiritual practices, while your parents adhere strictly to one faith.

- You advocate for modern and progressive political ideas, while your parents maintain more traditional views.

Step 3: Inquire About Ancestral Beliefs

1. **Discuss with Your Parents:** Engage in a heartfelt conversation with your parents about these differing beliefs. Inquire whether their parents (your grandparents) held similar views or if they experienced their own shifts in perspective. This will help you trace the generational threads of belief.

2. **Document Your Findings:** Record what you discover from these conversations, noting any patterns or recurring themes that arise.

Example:

- You embrace a more flexible parenting style, while your parents were strict disciplinarians.

- You explore various spiritual practices, while your parents adhere strictly to one faith.

- You advocate for modern and progressive political ideas, while your parents maintain more traditional views.

Step 4: Reflect and Integrate

1. **Analyze the Insights:** Reflect deeply on the shared and differing beliefs you've uncovered. Consider how these beliefs have shaped your identity and influenced your life choices.

2. **Decide on Changes:** With love and clarity, determine which beliefs you wish to continue nurturing and which ones you feel ready to transform or release. This conscious choice is a vital part of your healing journey.

3. **Create a Personal Action Plan:** Based on your reflections, craft a plan for integrating or changing these beliefs in your life. This might involve setting new personal intentions, adopting new practices, or continuing conversations with family members.

Through understanding and addressing these familial beliefs, you can cultivate deeper self-awareness, heal generational wounds, and create a more empowered and authentic path forward. Let this exercise be a beacon of grace and insight on your journey of ancestral healing.

Forgive Your Parents

Many of us are privileged to have grown up in nurturing homes, where our parents provided love and stability, enabling us to become who we are today. Most of us are truly grateful. However, not everyone can echo this sentiment.

At 19, I found myself kicked out of my home. Back then, it seemed like a catastrophe, but in hindsight, it was a pivotal turning point for the better. I'm convinced that, for the sake of our personal growth and our parents' continued development, it's beneficial for young adults to embark on their own journey as soon as they're legally able to. Now I am not saying this is the case for everyone as sometimes we have the privileges to be able to live with our parents for as long as we may be able to finish that specific cycle.

Let's acknowledge it: we all have our moments of youthful rebellion, constantly yearning for more from life. This isn't exclusive to us; our parents were once in the same boat. Imagine the seismic shift in their lives, the abrupt transition from their own adventures to the responsibilities of parenting!

When a young adult steps out into the world, it's not just a rite of passage for them. This transition also offers parents a precious chance to rediscover themselves, to explore new dimensions of life that might have been on pause. Enduring the rigors of parenting is a monumental achievement in today's world. When children leave the nest, it provides a unique opportunity for parents to rekindle their bond and refocus on their relationship. Often, you'll notice that relationships evolve, sometimes even falter, once the nest is empty.

Take moments to reflect: have you ever found yourself reacting to your parents or those who have greatly influenced your upbringing with surprisingly poor attitudes, only to immediately recognize that your response wasn't right? Almost as if you have a reactionary defense mechanism installed and coded towards them. Sometimes you might wonder, "I don't even speak to any of my friends this way. Why would I speak to someone whom I love most in this way?" This instinctual defensiveness often stems from unresolved emotions and memories lingering within us.

For instance, a friend of mine shared her experience of moving from Peru to the United States at the age of 9. When her mother had to leave her with her father and sister temporarily, she was engulfed by a profound sense of worry and longing for her mother's presence. From her mother's perspective, this separation was a sacrifice made out of love, a necessary step to secure a job and establish stability before bringing the whole family over for a new beginning. Despite her mother's intentions and the safety provided by a caring father, my friend harbored feelings of abandonment she never voiced.

Such experiences, though seemingly minor, highlight the importance of understanding and communication within a family. Unaddressed, these feelings can lead to a build-up of resentment, deeply rooting within us and affecting our interactions. In the spirit of healing and embracing a path of spiritual and emotional growth, it becomes essential to recognize and forgive these past hurts—not just for our parents' sake, but for our own. To forgive our parents is to understand the context of their actions and decisions, acknowledging that they, too, are navigating their own journey with its challenges and limitations. This doesn't mean forgetting or excusing hurtful behaviors but rather choosing to move forward with compassion and empathy.

In doing so, we open a space that may lead to a deeper connection and mutual understanding. This journey of forgiveness and understanding can be challenging, yet it is profoundly rewarding. In this journey of leaving and letting go, there's a profound space for growth, forgiveness, and a renewed commitment to the paths we choose to walk. This is due to being faced with the emptiness left in the wake of ritualistic episodes between siblings, the hustle and bustle of family living, and a perpetually growing laundry pile. For the first time in years, a couple is left alone in their own silence, and the growing gap between them, once filled with soccer practice, homework, and grocery lists, is suddenly brought up close and personal in the rawest way possible. Building a bridge back to one another is a labor of love and dedication.

"Grounding into my humanity, finding my way back to spirit"

Your Parents are Just People

In childhood, our parents may seem superhuman, all-knowing, and larger than life. At some point, we are all faced with the sobering reality that they are also beautifully flawed human beings experiencing life as we all are. They were placed in our lives to be our wisest teachers. When we allow our view of our parents to be led by empathy over anger, we liberate ourselves in the process.

Understanding that our parents once had dreams of what their lives would be like before they had us. Most of our parents were unable to move forward with these plans after they had us. Maybe your parents immigrated to another country for a better opportunity and were forced to take on jobs that were in conflict with their integrity, their potential, their dreams, or their pride—in order to give you a better life. Perhaps your mother harboured dreams of her art gracing galleries. Why not honor that unfulfilled aspiration by giving her a painting class?

This tendency of parents to guide us toward paths they themselves couldn't tread is not uncommon. Take my mother, for instance, who once dreamt of soaring through the air as a trapeze artist in the circus! Consequently, I found myself immersed in dance classes from the tender age of three, almost as if I was being primed for the circus myself!

If your bond with your parents feels fraught, I urge you to view them through a different lens. Try to see them not just as your parents but as individuals in their own right—as fellow beings under the Great Spirit, as friends, diligent colleagues, and genial neighbours. Recognize them as individuals who have experienced their own trials and tribulations, as once innocent children, perhaps as lovers who have faced disappointment, and, like all of us, as works in progress on a journey of growth and self-discovery.

Our elders embarked on their life paths from a different place than where we stand today, laying down a foundation through their lifetimes from which we benefit, granting us a more elevated starting point. As the cycles of life turn, it's natural for us to advance beyond our parents, nurturing the growth of our lineage. When you recognize this progression, embrace gratitude rather than resentment. Honor them by nourishing their inner spirit. Take them out for lunch at their favourite simple spots, cook for them, or better yet, explore the dreams of their youth. Perhaps your father once aspired to soar through the skies as a pilot. Why not give him the thrill of an aviation lesson?

Engage deeply with them. Ask about the memories of their younger days, their first brush with love, ask them how they feel love with your mother, ask them for their proudest achievements. Such conversations can unearth hidden talents and passions, revealing unhealed scars from their own ancestral ties. Understanding these wounds is like finding keys to long-sealed doors within your spirit, doors that lead to your own saga. This journey of healing extends beyond the immediate bonds of parent and child. It reaches out to aunts, uncles, and beyond. Reconnecting with these familial threads, acknowledging their past struggles, is a profound step towards mending your lineage.

This path of empathy and acceptance isn't solely about affection; it's a recognition of the shared essence that flows through you. Even in the face of challenges, remember that the very essence of your ancestors, encoded in your DNA, holds the potential to unlock realms of freedom and understanding, guiding you along a path of growth and liberation.

Generational trauma is a profound legacy we inherit from our ancestors, extending beyond the immediate lineage to include uncles, aunts, and distant kin. It's a shared history etched into our spirits, calling for our attention and healing to prevent its shadow from stretching into the future. In the spirit of wisdom passed down through the ages.

The initial step is recognizing the presence of ancestral trauma within us. This awareness opens pathways for meaningful dialogue with parents, grandparents, or any available ancestors, allowing insight into the lives they led before our time. Through these stories, a clearer perspective emerges, shedding light on our own experiences. It's about observing, reflecting, and discerning the patterns woven through generations, thereby gaining a deeper understanding of the forces that shape us.

Upon acknowledging the existence of these traumas, the mantle of responsibility rests on your shoulders. It's imperative to understand that it is your role to conclude these ancestral cycles. Failing to do so means the traumas inherited will cascade down to future generations. Thus, the journey of healing is not solely for your own liberation but also a gift to those yet to come, sparing them from the burdens that weighed upon you. Embracing this duty might involve forgiving your ancestors, seeking to truly understand their life stories, and recognizing that you possess the power to halt the perpetuation of these burdens.

Extend forgiveness and gratitude to your ancestors. It's essential to cultivate a heart of forgiveness towards your ancestors, encompassing parents, grandparents, and extended family members, who may have, knowingly or unknowingly, contributed to the trauma you carry. Recognize their humanity, their susceptibility to error, and understand that, had they possessed the awareness, they would not have wished these burdens upon you. Have you ever considered that maybe you had ancestors that took part in the destruction? The truth is we do not know on which side of the spectrum they were on. Equally important is the expression of gratitude for the positive legacies they've imparted. Acknowledge that your heritage is a tapestry of both light and shadow, and it's from this intricate blend that your unique journey is woven.

Embrace the understanding that in choosing to heal, you may stand apart, akin to the "black sheep" within your family circle. Traumas often manifest as deeply ingrained habits; choosing a different path, like abstaining from alcohol at family events, removing yourself from conflict, or breaking traditional life paths your family has taken, can set you apart. Similarly, pursuing therapy can be a solitary journey, especially if it challenges long-held family perceptions or traditions. Despite potential misunderstandings or criticisms from family members who may not see the need for such steps, it's crucial to stay strong. These challenges are part of the journey, marking significant moments when you might find yourself shifting away from established family norms.

Reflecting on my own childhood, I vividly recall discussions about the essence of boundless love and instinctively standing up for friends who were perceived as different. As I navigated my teenage years, I found a sense of belonging and duty in defending and befriending members of the LGBTQ+ community. My connection to this cause felt deeply personal, rooted in the stories my father shared about my Uncle Hernan Antonio Restrepo, who passed away in the '80s before I was born. My father often spoke of my uncle's love for painting, dancing, and travelling—passions we would have shared.

At 15, I learned more about Uncle Hernan's life. He was a pioneer in Cartagena, Colombia, courageously one of the first to openly embrace his homosexuality and, tragically, among the first known AIDS cases in the area. This revelation deeply moved me, making me feel as though I was destined to continue his legacy of courage and acceptance. Years later, following my grandfather's passing, as relatives focused on material possessions, I requested something different: a photograph of Uncle Hernan. Eventually, I placed his picture in a frame on the family altar, alongside my partner's guardians and my grandparents. Despite never meeting him, I questioned my actions, wondering about the appropriateness of honoring him in such a personal space.

In a moment of introspection, I prayed to Uncle Hernan, asking for a sign that he approved of my gesture and wished for me to keep his memory alive in my home. Shortly after, as if by divine synchronicity and the overwhelming powers of a WhatsApp chat that every Latin American family has, the first message I opened was one from my father celebrating the life of my uncle. Without knowing, I celebrated and honored my uncle's legacy on his very birthday, 45 years later. It was a clear sign that honoring and remembering him was not only accepted but celebrated. This concept extends beyond our direct lineage—parents and grandparents—to include aunts, uncles, and other relatives who have shaped the familial and energetic path we walk.

Purification: Making Space for Ancestral Wisdom

Our healing journeys often stir something deep within—a call to purge, to cleanse, to release. These urges, though at times unsettling, are an echo of ancestral wisdom guiding us back to balance. The act of decluttering, in all its forms, is more than a surface-level endeavor; it's a sacred ceremony, a bridge between the seen and unseen, the present and the past.

In the spirit of ancestral healing, purification becomes a way to honor those who came before us. It's an acknowledgment of their journeys, their sacrifices, and the wisdom embedded in their survival. Decluttering isn't just about letting go of things; it's about making space—space for the soul to expand, for clarity to emerge, and for the light to flow freely into the shadows.

Physically, the act is a ritual of release. Like the shedding of autumn leaves, it creates room for new growth and allows energy to circulate through the spaces we inhabit. Mentally, it calls us to sift through the layers of inherited beliefs and perceptions, questioning which narratives still serve us and which ones must be released. Emotionally, it's like tending a garden, pulling out the weeds of past wounds while nurturing the soil with forgiveness and grace.

This process of purification is deeply personal, as unique as the ancestral paths that brought us here. For some, it might look like clearing out a home filled with excess, while for others, it's about cherishing meaningful objects tied to family stories—like the antiques I hold dear, each piece a memory of my father and our shared adventures. Your sacred space might look entirely different—vibrant, bold, or eclectic. There is no one-size-fits-all; what matters is that it reflects your truth and allows your spirit to thrive.

As we declutter, we're not just removing the old; we're making room for the sacred. This act of letting go isn't about denying the darker aspects of ourselves but embracing them. The shadows are just as much a part of us as the light. When we accept this duality, we begin to harmonize, weaving together the threads of existence into something whole.

The wisdom of our ancestors also reminds us that healing is deeply intertwined with the spaces we inhabit. The environments they navigated shaped their resilience and ingenuity, and so too can a shift in environment inspire us. Stepping into a new setting, whether through travel, joining a new community, or simply rearranging your space, can shake us free from the chains of habit. It's like the first day of school—a little scary, yes, but filled with the promise of something new.

Changing your environment isn't about running away; it's about breaking patterns that no longer serve you. It's a chance to nurture new habits, create healthier routines, and rediscover yourself in ways you didn't know were possible. Whether it's a spiritual retreat, a pilgrimage, or a simple change in your daily routine, these shifts open doorways to transformation. They invite clarity, introspection, and the courage to step into your authenticity.

Astrocartography, for example, offers a unique lens to explore how the places we inhabit align with our personal energy. It's a modern map of ancestral wisdom, showing us where we might find love, success, or healing. But no matter where we go, the essence of transformation is rooted in what's inside us. Surrounding yourself with environments and people that reflect who you are and who you're becoming is one of the most profound acts of self-love.

Decluttering, changing environments, and engaging in spiritual journeys aren't just acts of personal growth. They're a way to honor those who came before us, to continue their legacy of resilience, and to pave the way for those who will follow. By creating space—within and around us—we allow the wisdom of the past to guide us toward a future filled with clarity, purpose, and harmony.

It's Not That Serious: Let It Be

Life has a way of making us feel like everything depends on us, like every little detail carries the weight of the world. But here's the truth: it's not that serious. When you zoom out and take the eagle's perspective, soaring above the chaos, you see life for what it is—a vast, interconnected journey where the things we often magnify into mountains are really just tiny pebbles. From this vantage point, you can let it be.

What feels insurmountable today is often a fleeting moment in the grand scheme of our lives. Even the darker experiences—grief, loss, change—are part of our earthly journey. Worries, most of them, are creations of the mind, shadows cast by fears that rarely manifest. The mind loves to blow things out of proportion, but when you shift perspective, those looming shadows shrink, and you see them for what they are: opportunities to grow, learn, and evolve.

Taking life less seriously doesn't mean you're dismissive or careless—it means you're free. Free to laugh when things don't go as planned, free to be vulnerable, and free to connect with life in its raw, unpolished beauty. Vulnerability, after all, isn't a weakness. It's the magic that cracks us open to authenticity and trust. It's the soil where deep connections grow, the kind that enriches life in ways you can't imagine when you're buried under seriousness.

Take a moment to reflect: what's your worry right now? Is it a bill that needs paying? Conflict at a job you don't love? Someone you care about falling ill? Maybe it's a spiraling thought about your partner out with friends, imagining the worst-case scenario where they meet someone better than you. Or maybe you're nervous about a big presentation at work and can already picture yourself tripping in front of the entire room. These worries pile up, filling your mind and stealing your peace.

But if you sit with them for a moment and strip them down to their core, you'll often find that they're just noise. And underneath it all, the biggest fear we all have to conquer is death itself.

Facing the Fear of the Worst-Case Scenario

The fear of death looms large, casting its shadow over many of our smaller fears. But what if confronting this fear head-on could set us free?

Write out the worst-case scenarios your mind loves to play on repeat. Sit with them. Let yourself feel their weight. Now, take a step back and ask: are these fears real, or are they just constructs of my mind? You'll likely find they're more imagined than tangible. The truth is, even when the worst does happen, you're stronger than you think.

Releasing these fears begins with recognizing them for what they are: shadows. They do not define you. They do not control you. By naming them, you take away their power.

Affirm Your Freedom

- "Now that I am free of the belief that I'm not good enough, I pursue my dreams with confidence and joy."

- "Now that I am free of the fear of failure, I take bold steps toward my goals."

- "Now that I am free of the fear of death, I embrace each day as a gift and live fully."

Let these affirmations be your guide, grounding you in the present and giving you the courage to move forward.

Transforming Fear into Trust

The fear of death—and the many smaller fears it spawns—can be a great teacher if we let it. It reminds us of what matters most: love, connection, and the legacy we leave behind. When we stop letting fear dictate how we live, we open ourselves to joy, growth, and deeper purpose.

Your life is not about the worries you carry or the fears you face. It's about how you move through them. Let death be a reminder—not a threat—that every moment is precious. Let your fears push you toward living boldly, loving deeply, and trusting in the beauty of your journey.

You are here for a reason, and every moment is an opportunity to honor that purpose. Release the fears that hold you back and affirm the life you want to create. You were not sent here to live in fear but to discover that within the shadow of death lies the light of living.

How Earth Breathes Through Us

The Earth is revered as the ultimate mother, the ancestor of all creation, the giver of life, and the final resting place for our physical forms. Her breath is intertwined with ours, a sacred cycle that sustains all beings. This deep connection to Mother Earth is a testament to the life force she shares with us, nourishing our bodies and spirits with her abundance.

Have you ever seen videos or pictures of Earth breathing? The sheer existence of our planet is an indescribable miracle. We are organisms housed by this great miracle that also needs to breathe like a newborn baby. Unlike a newborn baby, there's no parent to pray for the Earth's first breath.

Mother Earth, in her boundless generosity, sustains us, offering the richness of her soil and the healing embrace of her plants, ensuring our journey upon her is marked by wellbeing and harmony. As we inhale, drawing in the breath of life, it is as if the Earth herself breathes with gentle satisfaction. This act of breathing becomes a sacred exchange, a reminder of our deep connection and unity with her. It is through this understanding that we learn not just to exist alongside her but to live in respectful reciprocity, honoring the cycle of give and take that defines our relationship with the world.

We have a symbiotic relationship with plants, enabling us to work together. Herbs help us heal. Each herb creates medicine from its bark, seed, flower, or leaf, each from a different place. It's the essence of these plants that helps us energetically and physically. When you grab a plant and squeeze it, that oil that comes out is the essence or spirit of the plant. It is that essence that works on the mind, body, and spirit. The essence of the Earth is mirrored in the comforting presence of our human mothers, whose love and warmth are reflections of the greater maternal spirit that envelops us.

The plants, the children of Mother Earth, offer us their essences, imbued with healing vibrations and ancient wisdom. These plant essences, captured in essential oils, carry the frequencies of Earth's nurturing energy—like the rose's vibration of love, they speak to our beings, harmonizing our bodies and spirits. Ancient civilizations understood this connection, utilizing plant-based medicines to align with Earth's rhythms. These natural remedies, steeped in the intelligence of the plant kingdom, interact with our bodies in profound ways, reaching into our very cells to heal and restore. The act of breathing in these essences is a communion with Earth herself, a way to absorb her healing energies and recalibrate our inner balance.

Yet, in our fast-paced world, the simple act of breathing has been forgotten by many. To truly breathe is to engage in a sacred exchange with the Earth, to take in her life-giving air and return it, enriched by our own essence. Breathing should be an act of gratitude, a moment to connect deeply with the rhythm of life that pulses through us. Mother Earth has bestowed upon us an abundance of resources, each with the power to heal and sustain. It is our responsibility to honor these gifts, to engage with them mindfully and with gratitude. By doing so, we not only nourish ourselves but also participate in the greater cycle of giving and receiving that defines our relationship with the Earth.

When we breathe freely and with intention, we align our energies with those of Mother Earth, grounding ourselves in her strength and stability. This connection alkalizes our bodies, bringing us into harmony with the natural world and reminding us of our place within it. In this way, each breath becomes a prayer of thanks, a recognition of the boundless love and wisdom that Mother Earth offers us. As we walk this path, let us remember that to breathe is to engage in a sacred dialogue with the source of all life, a dialogue that nurtures, heals, and brings us home to ourselves.

Living in harmony with the land heals the roots of our family trees, mending the connection between past and present. By listening to the whispers of the Earth, engaging in her protection, and passing these values down through generations, we ensure that the circle of life continues unbroken, nourishing the bond between all living beings and the planet that sustains us. In this way, honoring Mother Earth is not just an act of preservation but a profound healing journey for our lineage, ensuring a future where the planet and its people thrive together.

To truly receive the medicine offered in this book, we must learn to ground ourselves deeply and offer back to our planet, nurturing the symbiotic relationship that sustains us all.

Prayer for Mother Earth, Madre Tierra, Pachamama

O Great Mother Earth, Madre Tierra, Pachamama, We stand humbly on your sacred ground, Grateful for the life you bestow upon all beings. You are the first mother, the giver of life, And the final resting place for our spirits.

With each breath we take, we feel your spirit within us, A sacred exchange that sustains our souls. In the laughter of flowers and the embrace of your plants, We honor the gifts you provide.

Thank you for holding us in your cradle, Safe in your arms like a child in the womb. We pray for your rivers to flow freely, Your mountains to grow stronger, And your deep blue oceans to remain pure.

May the fires that rage be tamed and gentle, Bringing renewal without destruction, So that your forests may thrive and your creatures find peace.

May we walk in harmony with you, Grounded in your strength, living with gratitude, Breathing in your essence, and returning it enriched. O Great Mother, we pledge to protect you and thank you always.

Activation for Code One:
Rooted with Ancestral Inheritance

The Earth is revered as the ultimate mother, the ancestor of all creation, the giver of life, and the final resting place for our physical forms. Her breath is intertwined with ours, a sacred cycle that sustains all beings. This deep connection to Mother Earth is a testament to the life force she shares with us, nourishing our bodies and spirits with her abundance.

Affirmations for Code One:

- I honor the wisdom and resilience of my ancestors, grounding myself in their strength.

- The legacy I carry within me guides and supports my journey.

- My roots are deep and unwavering, connecting me to my purpose.

Prompt to Reflect: As you walk forward, ask yourself, What legacy do I wish to leave for those who come after me? Imagine yourself standing among your ancestors, your dreams interwoven with theirs. What guidance might they offer you now?

CODE TWO

- Recreation & Rebirth Flow -

Embrace your past as the soil from which your future blossoms. Plant seeds of wisdom in the fertile ground of experience, cultivating a forward-focused mindset that transforms lessons into opportunities, and history into a foundation for a brighter tomorrow.

Code Two invites us to honor our roots as the fertile ground for new growth, transforming past wounds into wisdom. In this space, healing becomes an act of creation, where authenticity and self-expression paint the masterpiece of who we truly are. Trusting in Divine timing, we let go of control and flow with the natural rhythm, knowing that the right path will reveal itself. As we release the need to live by others' standards, we reclaim our power to shape a life rooted in joy and boundless potential. Now is the moment to step fully into this truth.

How Earth Breathes Through Us

The Earth is revered as the ultimate mother, the ancestor of all creation, the giver of life, and the final resting place for our physical forms. Her breath is intertwined with ours, a sacred cycle that sustains all beings. This deep connection to Mother Earth is a testament to the life force she shares with us, nourishing our bodies and spirits with her abundance.

Have you ever seen videos or pictures of Earth breathing? The sheer existence of our planet is an indescribable miracle. We are organisms housed by this great miracle that also needs to breathe like a newborn baby. Unlike a newborn baby, there's no parent to pray for the Earth's first breath.

The only command given to them was simple—to trust, to live in alignment with love, and to let go of the need to control what was already perfect. But when the serpent whispered, temptation took root. And with it came the fall: not just from grace but into fear, discipline, and the endless cycle of striving for what had already been given freely. The very fabric of bliss was exchanged for doubt, and humanity began its long forgetting.

We, too, have forgotten. We've mistaken busyness for purpose, suffering for growth, and scarcity for humility. We've imposed rules upon ourselves that were never written by the Divine. Yet, the echoes of Eden still whisper to us, calling us back to our original mission—the simplest and most profound one of all: to live in pleasure, to bask in the sweetness of being alive, and to love with unbridled authenticity.

Life is, and has always been, the ceremony. Every sunrise invites us to begin again. Every breeze reminds us of the gift of presence. And every moment we spend in peace, in true enjoyment, honors the very reason we were placed here.

To live in pleasure is not indulgence; it is alignment. It is remembering Eden—not as a story of loss but as a blueprint for what life can still be. It is reclaiming the knowledge that bliss is our birthright, that love is our natural state, and that to live without fear is the ultimate service to ourselves and to the world.

Step into this knowing. Witness life not as a series of obligations but as the sacred, unfolding ceremony it was always meant to be. Like Eve and Adam, look around you—not with the eyes of those cast out but with the heart of those invited in. Bliss is not a distant memory; it is a present choice. Choose it, and let the garden grow again within you.

Life is the Ceremony

Every day is a sacred gift, marked by the gentle rhythm of the sun and moon, faithfully guiding us through the passage of time. These celestial companions remind us of the constancy of nature, offering us new beginnings even amidst the chaos of the world. It's as though the universe itself whispers, "This is your Eden—your chance to live, love, and embrace the pleasures of this divine garden."

I've noticed a harmony, a quiet dance between the cosmos and our inner tides. As the celestial movements ebb and flow, they seem to mirror the rhythm of our spirits, nudging us to reassess, reflect, and embrace change. Like birthdays, they invite us to pause and honor the intricate patterns that make up our lives—the daily brushstrokes that create the masterpiece.

In a society so fixated on massive goals, bucket lists, and grand transformations, we often overlook the sacred beauty in the mundane. Life isn't just found in monumental moments or breakthrough achievements; it's in the way the wind feels against your skin, the way you stir your morning coffee, or the laughter shared at dinner. The ceremony of life is here—in every breath, every step, every heartbeat.

Why do we feel that urge to start over? To shave our heads in a symbolic Britney moment? To disappear into nowhere and rebuild from scratch? These longings aren't just dramatic cries for reinvention—they're echoes of a deeper desire to break free from mindless routines and rediscover vibrancy. But true reinvention doesn't require dramatic gestures. It's found in the way we bring intention into the smallest acts.

Recreation lives in the seemingly ordinary—the way you braid your hair, select your outfit, or sit quietly with yourself. These aren't just motions; they're sacred ceremonies. When infused with presence and intention, they become acts of self-love, ways of realigning with your highest self.

The flow state—true harmony—isn't about striving for grandiosity. It's about tapping into the joy of the present moment. It's the bliss in hearing birds at dawn, the nostalgia of a familiar scent, the peace of a solitary walk. These small, sacred moments weave the fabric of a fulfilling life.

Bliss isn't something we chase—it's something we uncover, hidden in plain sight, waiting in the pauses we so often overlook. When we lean into these moments, life stops being a race and starts becoming a ceremony. A sacred dance where the grand and the small merge seamlessly, teaching us that the greatest joy lies in simply being.

Life itself is the grandest celebration. Every day, every act, every breath is a ritual—a brushstroke on the canvas of existence, inviting us to embrace the fullness of who we are and the beauty of the world around us.

Give, Give, Give

Bliss isn't something we chase—it's something we uncover, hidden in plain sight, waiting in the pauses we so often overlook. When we lean into these moments, life stops being a race and starts becoming a ceremony. A sacred dance where the grand and the small merge seamlessly, teaching us that the greatest joy lies in simply being.

Forgiveness is more than just an act; it's an exchange, a gift of grace, understanding, and second chances. But we can't say "forgive" without "give"—they're intertwined, each essential to the other. So many of us are deeply giving by nature, often instinctively putting others first, eager to serve those we love, to provide for the less fortunate, to care for the Earth and its creatures. We give, thinking it's selfless, virtuous, and often, it is. But we forget that the flow of giving must always be balanced by a readiness to receive. Without this balance, we risk depletion, burnout, and even bitterness.

Consider how giving can become a defense mechanism, a way to avoid looking at our own needs. We might give our time, our energy, our love, all the while deflecting attention from ourselves. This deflection may even feel natural—after all, we're helping others, right? Yet, neglecting our own well-being in this way can erode our health, strain our nervous systems, and exhaust our spirits. We're here not just to give endlessly, but to accept in return. When we deny ourselves the right to receive, we disrupt the natural cycle of abundance. This isn't true selflessness; it's self-neglect, a kind of quiet selfishness that keeps us from the fullness of life.

The universe operates on a law of balance, where giving and receiving are intimately connected. For every act of giving, there is an invitation to receive—a restoration that fuels us to continue giving wholeheartedly. But how many of us resist this? We are quick to be there for others, to offer comfort, support, and a shoulder to lean on. Yet when it comes to receiving, we hesitate, feeling unworthy or fearing that it might make us "selfish." This resistance keeps us in a cycle of overextension, preventing us from the very nourishment we need to sustain our giving nature.

This code is often associated with sexuality, pleasure, and creativity. It's about more than just sensuality—it's about allowing ourselves to enjoy the fruits of life, the blessings we are meant to accept as much as we give. Receiving is a natural extension of giving; it's how we refill our wells, how we stay whole and joyful in our efforts to uplift others.

We see this imbalance vividly in people who struggle to leave toxic or abusive relationships. Often, the most giving souls end up in these situations, endlessly offering endless amounts of chances, believing in the potential of the other person. In these cases, they prioritize the needs of others so completely that they lose sight of their own worth. They've trained themselves to believe that sacrificing their own well-being is noble, yet this mindset traps them, diminishing their self-worth. Until they learn to receive respect, love, and care, they remain caught in cycles of self-sacrifice, unable to step fully into their own light.

When we finally open ourselves to receive, that's when true healing begins. The bruises and burdens of resisting life's blessings start to fade, and we allow ourselves to experience the abundance that was always meant for us. When we resist God's gifts, they can begin to feel like curses. We may start to resent the very people we sacrificed for or feel anger at the world. But when we open our hearts to both give and receive, life flows freely. Receiving isn't about selfishness—it's about honoring the cycles of life, letting blessings fill us so we can give from a place of wholeness, not depletion.

So, the next time we find ourselves giving, let's ask: Am I also willing to receive? Let us allow love, support, and abundance to enter our lives, trusting that by receiving, we are empowered to give even more generously. In this balance, we find true selflessness—the ability to share from a cup that is always full, overflowing with the richness of both giving and receiving.

The Magical Inner Child

Reflecting on childhood, I recall visiting family friends' homes and imagining them transformed by my boundless youthful creativity. I dreamed of vast pools, elaborate playrooms, and swing sets launching into my very own personal water park. The absence of trampolines in every adult living space seemed a mystery to me. I thought that's what adult money was for! I promised myself I'd never be a boring adult. I was resolute in crafting the life of my dreams when I grew up. I am sure you felt that exact same way.

Yet, here we are, living lives our younger selves would not be very proud of. Often as adults, we drift away from the imaginative core that flourished in our youth. We lose sight of the ability to mold our existence into the vision we once held so vividly. This forgetfulness dims the realization that we can indeed manifest the life we envisioned and become the beacon we yearned for in our earlier years.

Code two serves as a beacon, reigniting the reminder that the embodiment of your aspirations is not a distant dream. It's never too late, nor is it beyond your reach. You possess the innate capacity to sculpt your surroundings and, in tandem, reshape yourself.

By embracing these principles in our journey of recreation, we unveil a more refined version of ourselves, honoring the dynamic spirit of transformation deeply rooted in the wisdom of our ancestors. Remember, life itself is a ceremony of continuous creation and recreation.

To tap into your inner child and reconnect with the boundless creativity and imagination of your youth, consider integrating these simple yet profound activities into your daily life:

Adult Money for 'Childish' Joys: Allocate a small portion of your budget to something you would have adored as a child but might consider frivolous now—whether that's a trampoline, an elaborate set of water guns for epic battles, or even a day pass to a local amusement park. This act of spending on pure joy is a powerful statement that you haven't forgotten what makes you truly happy.

Daily Wonder Walks: Commit to a short weekly walk where you focus solely on observing the world with the wide-eyed wonder of a child. Notice the shapes of clouds, the colors of flowers, or the way shadows play on the ground. This practice helps you reconnect with the simple joys and curiosities that once filled your days.

Imaginative Role-Play: Spend an hour engaging in the role-play of what you wanted to be when you were a child. If you dreamed of being an astronaut, watch a documentary on space exploration in your homemade spacecraft (a fort made from blankets and pillows). If you aspired to be a chef, create a whimsical dish with no recipe, guided only by your taste buds and imagination.

Journal Prompts from Your Younger Self: Write down questions or prompts that your younger self might have asked you, such as "What adventures did you go on today?" or "What new thing did you learn?" Answer these at the end of your day to rediscover the curiosity and enthusiasm for life that characterizes childhood.

By incorporating these activities into your routine, you not only pay homage to the dreams and aspirations of your younger self but also weave a thread of playful creativity and joy through the tapestry of your adult life. This approach not only enriches your daily experience but also aligns you closer to the life you envisioned, fulfilling the promise of never becoming a 'boring adult.' Remember, the essence of recreation is not just about achieving lofty goals but rediscovering and embracing the whimsy and wonder that make life truly enchanting.

Wisdom from Your Inner Child

Grab an old photo of yourself as a kid and place it at your altar or somewhere you'll see it regularly. This isn't just about nostalgia; it's like a mini ceremony for your soul, reminding you of who you were before the world told you who to be.

Let this photo be a wake-up call to the real you—that fearless, curious kid who dreamed big without worrying about the "how." It's about tapping into that pure energy and finding clues about what really lights you up inside.

Seeing your younger self, think about what you loved and what made you excited. Maybe you wanted to be a doctor. Perhaps it wasn't about medicine but your deep drive to help people heal. That's a clue to what makes you, you. It's cool if life's taken you on a detour. The point is, you've got this unique gift, your own way to make a difference, even if it's just by being a great listener.

Your challenges aren't just obstacles; they're like secret maps to your passions. The stuff that's tested you the most could lead you to what you're meant to do. Opening up to this can light the way for others too, showing them it's possible to get through the tough stuff.

Now, think about who the little version of you needed by their side when they felt most alone or unheard. Imagine showing up for that child now, providing the support and understanding they craved. This exercise isn't just about reminiscing; it's about reawakening that part of you that was bold, curious, and unafraid to dream big. It's about reconnecting with your core self—the person you were before life's challenges tried to shape you into something else.

There are millions of versions of you out there, needing your help. The only challenge is you'll have to find them. They won't all look like kids anymore; they've grown just like you have. They might be at your workplace, in traffic, in the elevator, or online. Recognize that everyone carries their own inner child, often hidden beneath the layers of adulthood. By connecting with your own inner child, you can better empathize with others, understanding their struggles and dreams.

Your mission might just be the answer someone out there's been looking for. Big or small, your impact counts. So, as you chase what sets your soul on fire, remember that kid in the photo.

Stay true to them, and you're on your way to living a life that's not just successful, but meaningful.

Are you willing to push through to help them get to the other side? Your heart and purpose become not just your path but a light for others. When you show up for your inner child, you're also showing up for the world, offering the compassion, understanding, and support that everyone needs.

In the end, an open heart and purpose become not just your path but a light for others. As you navigate your journey, keep the image of your younger self close. Let it be a guide, a reminder of your true essence, and a source of inspiration to live authentically and passionately. By doing so, you not only honor your own journey but also illuminate the paths of those around you.

If you are interested in the guided meditation of this exercise please feel free to email my team at info@houseofvibration.com

The Art of Chill: Embracing Fluidity and Releasing Control

When I talk about being chill, I'm not just talking about staying calm under pressure or "playing it cool." It's deeper than that. It's about balancing life's messiness with grace—finding the space between chaos and calm where you feel steady, even when everything else feels like it's spinning. The people we admire for their chill aren't the ones who never deal with problems. They're the ones who handle them in a way that feels effortless, even when we know it's not. Being chill doesn't mean life hasn't hit you hard or that you've never had to pick yourself up. It means you've learned how to navigate those moments without letting them throw you off course completely. It's not about pretending things are fine when they're not or denying your emotions. It's about ownership. It's about authenticity. It's about understanding that not every reaction needs to come from a place of urgency. When you can look at life and say, "This moment isn't the whole story," that's real chill.

Let's get one thing straight: caring deeply about something doesn't mean you've lost your chill. It means you're human. Chill isn't about indifference—it's about being intentional with your energy. It's about staying grounded even when you're invested, trusting that what's meant for you won't miss you, and what doesn't align with you won't stay. Burnout happens when we confuse urgency with importance. Not everything demands immediate attention, and not every challenge needs to be met with maximum effort. Chill is about recognizing when to step in and when to let things unfold. It's about trusting your instincts and pacing yourself. Your spirit is boundless, but your energy isn't. Mastering chill is about reclaiming your calm, even when the world is testing you. That's where your real power lies.

The art of chill naturally draws people in because chill feels safe. It's that unspoken energy that says, "You belong here." Think about the people whose vibe makes you feel at ease. They're the ones who don't compete for attention or make you feel small—they welcome you as you are. That's what inclusivity is about. It's not just a buzzword; it's an energy that creates space for everyone at the table. True chill isn't exclusive. It's open-hearted and open-minded. It listens without judgment and values all perspectives. If you want to deepen your chill, start here: be the person who makes others feel seen and valued. That's the kind of energy people can't resist.

Chill isn't just a personality trait—it's a skill you can sharpen. It starts with learning how to ground yourself in the middle of life's chaos. Simple acts of self-care are powerful tools: sleeping in without guilt, cooking a meal just because it feels good, taking a long shower, or dancing like nobody's watching. These aren't just "nice-to-haves"; they're moments that reset your mind and reconnect you with yourself. Here's the thing: there's no such thing as a "bad trip" in life. It's all part of the journey. You have the power to take any situation, no matter how messy, and turn it into a lesson. That's the art of chill—transforming setbacks into stepping stones and moving through life with a calm, steady energy that can't be shaken.

Chill doesn't mean you've given up or you're slacking off. It's about intentionally choosing to slow down when life feels too fast. It's about reclaiming your time, your energy, and your peace. Some of the most important moments in life aren't the big, flashy ones. They're the quiet, slow ones—the ones where you let yourself breathe. They're the moments where you stop rushing and start enjoying. Chill isn't an escape from responsibility; it's a reset that lets you show up fully when it matters most.

True strength isn't rigid—it's fluid. When you embrace the art of chill, you stop trying to control everything and start flowing with life. That doesn't mean you're passive or careless. It means you're intentional. You're rooted in your values and your purpose, but you're flexible enough to adapt when things don't go as planned. By learning to let go and trust yourself, you master the art of navigating life with a steady hand and an open heart, ready to embrace whatever comes your way.

Detaching Yourself:

It's often said that adopting a playful approach to life might make it appear as though we don't take ourselves seriously. Yet, this perspective overlooks the profound truth that playfulness can coexist with depth and sincerity. Consider the act of playing an instrument, like the piano. When musicians are in their element, perhaps during a relaxed gathering with family and friends, their fingers dance over the keys with a natural, joyful ease. In these moments, uninhibited by formal expectations, they often create the most beautiful and soul-stirring melodies. The music born from such playfulness carries a spirit that formal performances, often laden with pressure and seriousness, struggle to match. This illustrates a core principle revered in our traditions: play is not the antithesis of importance. Engaging in our activities with a light heart does not strip them of their significance. Instead, it invites a spirit of joy and authenticity, allowing us to connect deeply with our tasks and with each other, echoing the harmonious balance that nature itself exemplifies.

Mastering the art of chill means stepping back to see the broader perspective. It involves recognizing that life's challenges and triumphs are part of a larger game. This isn't to trivialize life but to understand that many worries will fade in time. It's a logic game where maintaining balance among your elements is crucial. Know what energizes you, and what throws you off balance. Remember the importance of staying grounded. True logic and clarity come from being firmly rooted.

Identifying genuinely chill individuals has been enlightening. Those who embody chillness are effortless to be around, open-hearted, and able to detach from everything, embracing the present and being authentic. Speaking with younger individuals about who they consider cool might highlight the most popular figures, who aren't always the kindest. This reflects how coolness has been confused with popularity, obscuring the simplicity and joy of genuine coolness—being true to oneself. Consider whether you maintain your cool without external factors. Beyond the material—clothes, cars, jobs—what remains? Are you still cool on your own? True coolness comes from self-knowledge and being at peace with who you are at your core.

To truly embrace chillness, begin with self-reflection. The person who stands out isn't the one with the most attention or the flashiest lifestyle but the one who has mastered being at peace with themselves in any circumstance. Following the essence of finding bliss within, it becomes clear that the individuals who truly inspire us are those who embrace life's simplicity and authenticity. These are people who aren't afraid to play with dirt, demonstrating their willingness to engage with the world in its rawest form. They exhibit agility, nobility, and honesty in their actions, values that resonate more deeply than superficial success.

Reflect on the people you've met who, despite their financial success and ability to afford a luxury lifestyle, choose to sit in general admission with the crowds, dress in sweatpants, and wear Converse, and converse with the people. This choice is a statement of identity and belonging. It signifies a detachment from societal expectations of status and a movement towards genuine self-expression.

Being inspired by such individuals encourages us to let go of any preconceived notions of what defines us. It's about being inclusive, welcoming those who feel like outsiders, and creating a space where everyone feels valued. Embracing this approach means seeing people for who they are, beyond their external successes or failures, and applying the same non-judgmental perspective to ourselves. This liberation from expectations and societal norms frees us to live more authentically. It's in this space of acceptance and inclusivity that true inspiration lies. By embodying these values, we not only inspire others but also discover a deeper sense of fulfillment and connection within our own lives.

The Flow of Feminine Energy: Releasing Control

From the days of Eve, we, as humans, have carried the duality of creation and resistance within us. Eve's story often symbolizes the tension between trust and the desire to control—a tension born not from our nature but from centuries of conditioning. For women, this desire to control has a deeper root.

It was indoctrinated by being controlled. For centuries, women have faced oppression, manipulation, and systematic control, made to believe we were the cause of injustices, the root of disorder. This lie has woven itself into our subconscious, creating a constant need to grip tightly to every aspect of our lives as a means of survival.

But deep within, our essence tells a different story. Women are like water—naturally fluid, adaptive, and endlessly creative. Water doesn't resist; it flows. It doesn't cling; it molds to the container of life and, in doing so, shapes the world. This energy isn't weakness; it's power.

And yet, this fluidity, this flow of feminine energy, is not exclusive to women. Men, too, can access and embody it. Masculine energy, often associated with structure, protection, and action, thrives in balance with feminine energy—adaptability, creativity, and surrender. Both energies exist within all of us, and when men embrace their own fluidity, they unlock a deeper connection to intuition, creativity, and grace, balancing their strength with adaptability.

Control and willpower, however, are not the same. Control stems from fear—the need to force an outcome, to grip tightly because of distrust or insecurity. Discipline, on the other hand, is rooted in intention. It's the conscious act of directing energy without letting it consume or dominate you. This distinction is especially crucial when it comes to the most powerful energy within us: kundalini energy—the serpent energy that resides at the base of the spine, often awakened through spiritual practices or heightened awareness.

Kundalini energy represents pure potential, creation, and transformation, often tied to sexual energy because it is the source of both physical life and creative power. Women, in particular, may struggle with this energy due to centuries of being told our sexuality was dangerous, shameful, or something to be controlled by others. Over time, this narrative made many of us internalize control, repressing our fluidity, spontaneity, and even our pleasure.

When kundalini energy begins to rise, it can feel overwhelming, as if it's consuming you. Left unchecked, it can manifest through impulsive actions, overindulgence, or cycles of distraction. But this is where discipline—not control—becomes essential. Discipline allows us to guide the rising energy with intention, moving it through the chakras to fuel creativity, love, and purpose rather than letting it stagnate or overpower us.

When we embrace discipline, we honor our innate power without suppressing it. Kundalini energy, when directed, becomes a force of liberation—not just physical but spiritual, mental, and emotional. It reconnects us to our sacred essence, allowing us to reclaim what centuries of oppression sought to take: our ability to flow freely, to create, to experience life's pleasures, and to exist unapologetically in our divine power.

This is not just a journey for women. Men, too, benefit from balancing control with surrender, structure with fluidity. Masculine energy is strengthened—not diminished—when complemented by feminine flow. For both, the key lies in understanding that true power comes not from grasping but from guiding, not from controlling but from channeling.

Every time you feel the need to cling tightly, remember: your power is not in holding on but in your ability to flow and direct. Women, the desire to control was never yours—it was planted in you by systems that sought to oppress you. Reclaim your natural state of flow. Men, let go of the need to constantly "have it together" and discover the strength in surrender.

When you release control and embrace discipline, life transforms. The rising kundalini energy fuels your highest self, unlocking creativity, intuition, and bliss. The universe begins to move with you, and you'll find that life's unpredictability isn't something to fear—it's something to embrace. Together, we can reclaim the balance that was always ours and flow in the harmony of creation.

"Flowing will get you places forcing never could"

Worry 'Bout You, Be Happy

Let's get one thing straight: being at bliss isn't some luxury for the lucky—it's the most fundamental gift you can give yourself. Living a life filled with joy is the highest form of self-love, a bare necessity for the soul. Yet, so many of us get wrapped up in external responsibilities and the noise of the world that we forget the simplest truth: peace starts within. Sure, it's tempting to dive into the mysteries of life and untangle the chaos around us, but before any of that, the first step is choosing joy.

Happiness isn't a destination; it's a state of being. It's not something you chase—it's something you choose, every single day. And here's the kicker: peace isn't something you find outside of yourself; it's something you activate within. You don't have to fake it till you make it or slap a smile on a broken heart. Real joy isn't ignorance. True bliss comes from awareness—seeing things as they are, understanding your place in it all, and making peace with it.

Before you go running off to fix the world—or your friends, your family, or whoever's in your orbit—pause. Master yourself first. Get intimate with your own inner codes. Navigate your personal journey with grace, wisdom, and a sense of humor, because let's be real, the messiest parts of life are often the funniest in hindsight.

Now, let me say this: I've noticed something about people who get consumed by conspiracy theories and grand narratives. A lot of times, these are folks who feel deeply unsettled in their own lives. Maybe they're stuck at home, stagnant, dissatisfied, or struggling with personal issues they haven't yet faced. Instead of turning inward, they point outward, spinning tales about pink alien governments or shadowy overlords controlling their destiny. It's not that questioning the status quo is bad—hell, it's necessary sometimes—but when it turns into harming others or spreading fear, that's a red flag that the real battle might be internal.

So before you get tangled up in the world's chaos, nurture your well-being. Find your peace. Cultivate your joy. You don't need to solve every mystery to feel fulfilled. When you're on solid ground, with a clear mind and a joyful heart, you'll be ready to tackle the bigger issues—whether they're societal problems or, who knows, maybe chasing down a secret alien cabal.

Here's the thing: happiness isn't about plastering on a fake grin or pretending the hard times don't exist. It's about facing the challenges, embracing the chaos, and finding peace in the midst of it all. Joy is born from creativity—the kind that flows from your soul when you're connected to your true essence. It's about engaging with life as it is, not as you think it should be.

And let's teach this to the next generation. Happiness isn't in shiny objects or fleeting moments; it's in the authentic experiences that make life rich. The best moments are often the ones we overlooked when we were younger, those little joys we come back to as we grow.

Life isn't just about "being happy." It's about living fully—feeling every emotion, embracing every experience, and knowing that the hard times are just chapters, not the whole story. When you brush aside the pain or try to rush through it, it lingers in the shadows. Be present, even in the struggle. That's how you transform it.

Happiness isn't the endgame; it's the foundation. When you say, "I just want to be happy," you might be missing the bigger picture. Your purpose is larger than that—it's about dreaming bigger, moving with intention, and making a mark on the world. Joy and peace are just the launchpads, the calm centers from which we step into the beautiful chaos of life.

Not being happy with the way your life is isn't a flaw; it's a call to tap into your creativity. You have the power to shape your joy, your purpose, and your impact, no matter your circumstances. Happiness starts with you, but it's meant to be shared. When you broaden your vision to include the lives you touch and the world you help create, happiness transforms into something even greater—a ripple of bliss that carries us all forward.

You'll never find yourself

Understand you were created as an ever-changing, evolving child that was never meant to be done growing. The journey of self-recreation often uncovers new passions, goals, and paths that are more aligned with your spiritual values. This renewed sense of purpose can invigorate your spiritual practice, leading you to explore new facets of spirituality and how they integrate into your daily life. It can transform your actions into expressions of your deepest beliefs and values.

Quit trying to find yourself—instead, create yourself. To recreate yourself, you have to love the person you have become up until this moment. Give yourself grace and be proud of the little YOU that has come this far and has accomplished this life! Find value within yourself. The fact that you are looking to recreate yourself is a brilliant idea, and it comes from within you. This means that you've decided that you have enough value inside of you to go recreate.

Let go. To accept and embrace yourself, you do not need to understand everything. Let go of the idea of who you should or used to be. Repeat after me: "I love who I have created up until this moment. This is my story." Learn to give yourself credit when it's due. Acknowledge how far you've come mentally, spiritually, and physically. Now it's time to make space for the new.

I think the human urge to conceptualize and structure time speaks to our desire for these ritualistic checkpoints. "New Year, New Me" is a ritual we practice each year with the intention of leaving behind the things that no longer serve us so we can step forward on our path toward our goals. And sure, we don't always follow through with everything we set out to achieve, but there is something about the optimism and collective intention for betterment around this time of year that's magical to me.

We aren't just working with the universe; we are part of it. We need to be in tune with both parts of our polarity. Women should be in tune with their masculine energy. This is the aspect of self that brings us stability, grounding, and security in practical terms. It is equally important for men to be in tune with their feminine side as well, even though it's sadly rejected with more frequency this way around.

The feminine is the aspect of self from which our creativity comes, our intuition, our inspiration, our emotional safety, and expression. That's your sacral chakra. Chakras are energy points that are aligned with our bodies. When we embody our feminine, we strengthen our capacity to follow the flow of our process with more flexibility and openness so that we're able to download inspired guidance with receptivity. Our masculine then brings that inspiration into practical action, manifesting our divine wisdom into physical form earthside.

"The Universe will not allow you to move forward until you appreciate the present moment"

"You are the medicine"

Celebrate the Wins: Quit Preparing and Savor the Creation

We spend so much time preparing for the next big thing—planning, fixing, striving—that we forget to stop and honor the beauty of where we are. Life isn't just about the next goal or the next milestone; it's about pausing to recognize the magic of what you've already created. You've been on a journey, and every step you've taken deserves acknowledgment, no matter how small it may seem.

As you stand at the threshold of your next chapter, take a moment to breathe and look back. Celebrate the path you've walked. Celebrate the hard conversations you've had, the skills you've learned, and the times you showed up when it wasn't easy. Wins don't have to be grand to be worthy of celebration. They are found in the quiet moments of perseverance, the new perspectives you've gained, and the ways you've grown into yourself.

Before you rush into "what's next," quit preparing for just a moment and sit with the power of your own creation. Reflect on everything that brought you here—not to dwell, but to honor it. Too often, we get so caught up in "what's next" that we miss the opportunity to revel in the now. It's in this space of gratitude and reflection that you connect most deeply with yourself and your journey.

When you take time to celebrate, you're not just marking the wins—you're creating space to release what no longer serves you. Use this moment to let go of the doubts, the fears, and the old stories that weigh you down. Whether it's negative self-talk, unnecessary guilt, or the need for constant perfection, leave it behind. Let this be your reset.

And as you release, remember to ground yourself in gratitude. Gratitude isn't just about being thankful for what you have; it's about recognizing your own power to create. You've built something beautiful, and that deserves to be celebrated. Write a letter to your future self, not as a list of things to fix, but as a love note to who you're becoming. Speak to yourself with kindness and clarity, setting intentions that honor your deepest desires—not vague resolutions, but real, tangible visions for your life.

Life isn't just about the hustle; it's about the art of creation. And creation isn't a final destination—it's a journey, a process, a ceremony. You are both the creator and the masterpiece, constantly evolving, constantly becoming. So, pause. Celebrate. Let your wins fill you with joy and your setbacks teach you grace.

The next step will come, but for now, sit with what you've built. Let it remind you that you're capable of so much more than you give yourself credit for. You're not just preparing for a life you hope to live someday—you're living it now. Celebrate that. Honor that. And from this place of gratitude and recognition, step boldly into whatever comes next.

Activation for Code Two: Recreation & Rebirth Flow

This code called you to infuse intention into the rituals of your everyday life, transforming the mundane into the sacred. Through Code Two, you're reminded to release expectations, inviting playfulness and a return to that imaginative spark of childhood.

Affirmations for Code Two:

- I transform my daily routines into rituals that honor my essence.

- I release expectations, welcoming renewal and creativity in my life.

- My inner child guides me to a place of authenticity and boundless joy.

Reflective Question: Ask yourself, How can I nurture my inner child and bring playfulness into my daily life? Think about a small action you can take each day that sparks joy and reconnects you with that creative energy.

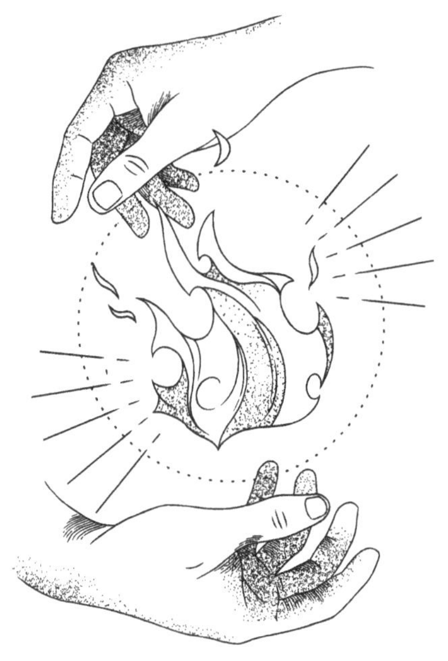

CODE THREE

- Leadership Frequency -

We cannot change that which we don't acknowledge.

Healing the solar plexus chakra is a sacred journey of transcending the ego and releasing false illusions of control. In this transformative process, we make space to embody our authentic strength, elevate self-esteem, and gracefully shift from power plays to conscious, heart-led leadership – a dance of empowerment that resonates with the harmony of our truest selves."

The Quiet Impact

Have you ever paused during a live performance to watch the performers command the crowd, their energy weaving an invisible thread that ties every soul in the room together? It's electric, magnetic—art in motion. That same energy, that same ability to inspire and connect, lives within each of us. Leadership isn't about commanding adoration; it's about creating a resonance so profound that others feel seen, heard, and moved as if your words, art, or actions speak directly to their soul.

An artist's role goes beyond the act of creating. It's about forging a connection so deep it's felt rather than seen. A true leader, much like an artist, feels the collective pulse—the silent stories, hopes, and struggles carried by those they guide. When you share your talents, your light doesn't dim. It spreads, like one candle igniting another, illuminating paths not just for yourself but for everyone around you.

The same way you've been inspired by a performer, there's someone out there inspired by you—and maybe not in the way you'd expect. Inspiration doesn't require recognition or knowledge. It's like the sun—it doesn't shine to be thanked; it simply burns. If you told the sun how much you loved him, his response would be, *"I'm simply here to burn inside of you."*

Think about it: have you ever been in a supermarket and noticed someone who caught your attention? Maybe it wasn't anything specific—perhaps it was the way they dressed, the way they smelled, or the way they interacted with their partner. They seemed effortlessly cool, or maybe not at all, but they stuck in your mind. Then, you see them again at the checkout line. You glance at their basket and think, *"They have good taste. Maybe next time I'll try that."* That person inspired you without ever knowing it.

Or maybe you're scrolling on social media, and the most random person shares a song. You hit play, and suddenly that song becomes your favorite. It shifts your mood, brightens your day. They'll never know the impact they had on you. That's the thing about inspiration—it's not always loud or intentional. It's subtle, organic, and deeply human.

This is your *solar plexus energy, your lemon glow.* It's the principle implanted in you at birth—the understanding that you are inspiring, teaching, and leading others, often without realizing it.

It's not about trying to shine; it's about being—living authentically, unapologetically, and fully.

The Silent Power of Your Frequency

As a leader, consider the energy you bring into every space. What's the essence of your frequency? Is it one of harmony, strength, and understanding? Leadership isn't just about words; it's about the silent power of your presence. Your energy speaks louder than your voice, shaping every interaction and every connection you make.

The same way you've noticed someone in passing, someone else is noticing you. It might not be your words or your actions; it could simply be your energy, your aura, or the way you carry yourself. You never know whose day you're brightening just by being you.

Leadership is not a smooth path. Success isn't just a celebration; it's a journey with trials, triumphs, and everything in between. Promotions, new relationships, or milestones in your craft aren't the end—they're the beginning of new challenges. True maturity as a leader isn't just about recovering from setbacks; it's about holding success with grace, staying grounded, and sharing the wisdom you've gained.

Leadership is not about asserting control—it's about staying aligned. A true leader doesn't cling to power or perfection. They act as a steady presence, a guide who honors the wisdom of the past and holds space for the present. Leadership is about balancing the weight of responsibility with the lightness of vulnerability. Vulnerability isn't weakness; it's a strength that connects us, allowing others to trust and follow with open hearts.

The leaders we admire most often aren't the ones with the flashiest achievements. They're the ones who remain resilient, who embrace life's pains alongside its joys, and who aren't afraid to show their humanity. It's their authenticity—their willingness to share their struggles and triumphs—that inspires us. They remind us that leadership isn't about being invincible; it's about being real.

A true leader is a protector, embodying the nurturing spirit of those who came before us. This doesn't mean shielding others from every hardship but creating a space where they feel safe and supported. Protection isn't about power—it's about presence. It's about being someone others can rely on, a constant amid life's uncertainties. This kind of leadership builds trust, strengthens communities, and fosters growth.

Leadership also requires foresight. Think of the spider weaving her web—not in haste or only when needed but with care and intention, preparing for what's to come. This proactive wisdom is at the heart of true leadership. A great leader doesn't just react to challenges; they anticipate them, crafting strategies and solutions with precision. They communicate these insights clearly, guiding their community with confidence and care.

Code there teaches us about ownership—of our truth, our power, and our ability to inspire others even when we think no one is watching. Leadership is about making fast, logical decisions, not for recognition but for the greater good. It's about taking healthy risks, not just for yourself but for humanity. It's about staying aligned with your purpose, letting your actions ripple out to elevate and connect others.

A leader doesn't quit when things get hard; they step back only when something no longer aligns with their truth. Leadership is a profound responsibility, but it's also an honor—a role we all carry in some way, whether for a crowd, a family, or ourselves.

So ask yourself: What frequency do I emit as a leader? Is it a frequency that uplifts and connects? Does it inspire others to move, create, and grow? Leadership isn't a title or a task. It's a frequency, a vibration, a presence.

Lead with grace, with courage, and with the unwavering belief that your light—your lemon glow—when shared, can illuminate the world. Remember, like the sun, your role is not to demand recognition but to burn brightly, inspiring others simply by being, you kinda don't have a choice but to shine sunshine.

> "Inspiring others is not about being looked up to, it's about being a reflection to others from a space that looks achievable."

Divine Time

I like to believe that the things we deeply want—when they truly serve us—want us back even more. It's not just wishful thinking; it's a pull that feels magnetic, undeniable, and intricately tied to our purpose. Whether it's people, opportunities, lifestyles, or experiences, those desires are not random. They are invitations from life, reminding us of what's possible when we're brave enough to align with them.

Here's the thing: it's not about chasing or forcing those things to happen. That energy will always keep what you want just out of reach. True manifestation isn't about hustle or grind. It's about alignment. It's about holding a vision so deeply and unapologetically that it becomes part of who you are. That vision transforms how you show up, the decisions you make, and the energy you carry. It's not about doing the most—it's about moving with intention, clarity, and faith.

When we align with divine timing, we tap into a universal truth: what is meant for us will not pass us by. But let's be clear—divine timing isn't passive. It's not sitting back, crossing your fingers, and hoping for the best. Divine timing is active trust. It's the sweet spot between allowing life to flow and being laser-focused on your path. It's waking up every day with the question: "Does this serve more than just me? Does this benefit mankind?" Because when what you want aligns with a higher purpose, the momentum shifts. The universe responds. Doors open.

And let's address resistance. We live in a world where everyone loves to say, "Rejection is redirection." Sure, it's a cute mantra, but it's often a cop-out for giving up too soon. When you're truly aligned with something, when you've asked yourself those deeper questions and know it's bigger than just you, you don't stop at the first "no." You don't crumble under criticism or resistance. You push through, holding the belief that "Objection is not rejection."

Objections are part of the process. They're not signs to quit; they're reminders to refine your approach, tighten your focus, and double down on your faith. They're the universe asking, "How bad do you want this?" And if you want it—if you know in your soul that it's for you—you keep moving. You adjust, pivot, and show up anyway, knowing that every step is taking you closer.

Divine timing is a dance. It's the rhythm between trust and action, surrender and determination. It's not about controlling every detail or forcing the outcome. It's about believing so fully in what you want that the universe has no choice but to deliver it. Because here's the truth: what you seek is already seeking you. The real question is, are you ready to meet it halfway?

And yet, there's a modern myth we've all fallen for: **"I don't have time."**

Let's call it what it is—a socially acceptable lie. We've turned busyness into a badge of honor, a way to prove our worth in a world that values productivity over presence. But the truth is, this constant hustle disconnects us from what truly matters. Telling ourselves, "I don't have time," is like willingly carrying a heavy stone. It blocks the flow of our energy, leaving us overcommitted and drained.

The ego loves busyness because it craves recognition. It thrives on the illusion that being busy equals being important. But let's flip the script. Instead of saying, "I don't have time," try, **"I'm honoring my current commitments."** Or, **"My energy is focused elsewhere, but I value this and want to revisit it later."** These phrases don't shut doors—they create space. They show respect for your priorities and invite understanding.

Time is not something to fight against. It's a river that flows naturally, and we shape its course with intention and discipline. A mentor once told me, **"Mastering time isn't about cramming every moment with tasks. It's about creating space for what truly matters."** By making space, we transform time from a relentless force into a gentle current that carries us toward what we truly desire.

When an opportunity comes your way, don't default to, "I don't have time." Instead, say, **"This is amazing, but my focus is elsewhere for now. Can we connect next week?"** This approach not only honors your current priorities but also keeps the door open for future possibilities. It's not just about time management—it's about nurturing relationships and showing up with intention.

Time isn't just about the clock ticking. It's the rhythm of life, the interplay between our purpose and our priorities. Family, work, community—these aren't burdens; they're the threads weaving your story. By approaching time with respect and alignment, you move from a mindset of scarcity to one of abundance.

And here's the paradox: the more you do, the more energy you generate. Action creates momentum, and momentum fuels energy. Movement doesn't deplete you—it feeds you.

So, embrace the flow. Let go of the need to control every second. Trust that divine timing is at work, even when life feels chaotic. Find beauty in the imperfections, humor in the unexpected, and grace in the process. Everything is unfolding as it should, in its own perfect time.

Repeat this Mantra:

I make time for prayer.
I make time to answer.
I make time for those I love.
I make time for my community.
I make time for rest.
I make time to notice.
I make time for creation.
I make time to process.
I make time for my body.
I make time to listen.
I make time to breathe deeply.

The Courage to Make Decisions

When I reflect on my teenage years, I often revisit moments that still hold weight—times when I was swept into situations I didn't want to be in, knowing better but staying silent. I can vividly recall hitchhiking with my friends more times than I care to admit, catching rides with older boys who seemed cool at the time or, worse, grown men who had no business giving rides to teenage girls. What lingers most isn't the rides themselves but the absence of courage to speak up and say, "No, I don't feel right about this."

Looking back, I see how divine intervention, or maybe just sheer luck, seemed to step in for me. God, or something greater, saved me from what could have been far darker outcomes. But even in those precarious moments, there were flickers of courage—small yet powerful—when I found the strength to change the course of what could've been my worst decisions.

I remember one night in particular. We were 14, planning to sneak out to a house party. My mother was strict, so anytime I wanted to go out, I had to tell her I was sleeping over at my best friend's house. That evening, as my mom was about to drop me off, I called my friend to ask what had become our standard pre-party question: "How are we getting there?" This was before Uber, back when we relied on hoping the party was on Collins so we could catch the S bus or a ride from someone's older cousin.

When my friend replied, "The same guys who gave us a ride home last night," something inside me froze. I instantly knew I couldn't do it. These weren't just random guys—they were total creeps. The night before, they'd pulled out a bottle of Xanax and said, "If you hang out with us again, we'll have a good time." That was my red flag. I told my mom I didn't feel like going anymore, a decision that felt so small at the time but turned out to be life-changing.

The next morning, I woke up to a storm of missed calls from my friend's parents, frantic and asking if I'd seen their daughters. When I finally got through to someone, I found out what I'd feared: that ride ended in the worst way imaginable for my friends—a loss of innocence that no child should ever endure. I never asked too many questions; I didn't want the details. But that moment marked me.

That decision—to stay home—saved my life. It taught me the value of listening to my inner voice, the one that knew better. I didn't fully understand it then, but I was beginning to cultivate the courage to be clear about what I wanted and, more importantly, what I didn't want. I didn't want to fall into manipulation or be led into rooms I never asked to be a part of.

On the other side of this story, there's another memory that makes me laugh. I had a close friend, and we were known for being bossy little brujitas. We were unapologetic about walking out of places that didn't vibe with us, leaving people wondering where we'd gone. If someone asked us what we wanted to do, we never said, "I don't know." That would've been a lie—we always knew. And so do you.

When you give up your voice to please others, you surrender the willpower of your path. You put yourself in situations that feel wrong but stay out of fear or obligation. That's when manipulation creeps in—when you let go of your boundaries for the sake of avoiding discomfort. But what's on the other side of avoiding confrontation? Resentment. When you don't confront the elephant in the room, that energy doesn't disappear; it festers. It rots, leaving bitterness and regret in its wake.

The courage to make decisions is about more than just saying no—it's about saying yes to yourself. It's about standing firm in your truth, initiating tough conversations, and sitting with the awkward silences that come with them. It's about not being afraid to call things out when they feel off or to leave spaces that don't align with your spirit.

Nowadays, whenever I'm interviewing someone or collaborating, one of my first questions is: **When was the last time you initiated a hard conversation?** If their response is, "I can't really remember" or "I try to avoid those situations," I immediately know this person isn't aligned with what we're doing. But when someone can immediately detail how they initiated a hard conversation, I see courage, emotional intelligence, and initiative.

For me, this ability is a marker of alignment. It shows someone who's not afraid to step into their truth, even when it's uncomfortable. Because that's what courage is—it's not the absence of fear but the willingness to face it. And in a world that constantly tests our boundaries, that kind of courage is priceless.

Authentic Confidence

We all seem to chase confidence as if it's some elusive destination. Yet the tricky part is this: you *can* never truly tell if someone is confident. What you can sense is whether their confidence is rooted in self-awareness and authenticity or if it's a mask propped up by ego and external validation. Authentic confidence is about embracing your true self—fully and unapologetically.

I grew up surrounded by a long line of beautiful women. To me, they were the epitome of femininity—drop-dead gorgeous, blonde, tan, fit, and always impeccably dressed. But as a little girl in a room full of poised Sleeping Beauties, I felt like Snow White. I was shorter, paler, and couldn't stop giggling to save my life.

My family loved dancing—salsa, booty dancing to El General, belly dancing—you name it, our living room turned into a club on Saturday nights But I wouldn't step into the middle of the room. Not because I didn't love to dance or didn't dance well enough, but because I didn't feel confident in my looks. And let's be honest, my belly was never flat enough to rock a two-piece with confidence.

That all changed when I was 17, during a psychedelic trip that stretched over two days. Let me tell you, that trip stripped me of all the stories I'd been telling myself. It hit me like a lightning bolt: I had stopped doing all the things I loved—not because I didn't enjoy them, but because I didn't think I was "visually up to par" with some imaginary standard.

This is what I see in so many of my clients. They have these incredible dreams, these deep-seated gifts they want to share, but they block themselves with the lie that they're not ready. I hear it all the time:

"I'll start when I quit my job… when I pay off my debt… when I move out… when I graduate… when I lose the weight… when I look the part… when I have the time."

Here's the truth: *you will never feel 100% ready.* Readiness isn't a requirement; it's a myth. What you do have is the authentic drive of desire right now.

When I started House of Vibration, I knew I wanted to focus on soul-driven leaders. I didn't want to fall into the traditional categories of business consulting, finance, or sales because my work wasn't about spreadsheets—it was about spiritual transformation. At the same time, I didn't want to be boxed into the "wellness brand" space. But let me be real—this was tricky because I kept ending up at wellness events. And as someone who's always been on the thicker side, the doubt crept in: *What are these pilates influencers going to think when I show up?*

But here's the thing: I'm not here to teach pilates. I was sent here to teach abundance, mindset, and spirituality—to show others how to align their inner world with their highest mission. My confidence didn't come from fitting into their mold; it came from showing up as my authentic self and knowing I had a message to share that could transform lives.

Nobody is out there doing what *you* are doing, in the way you are doing it. You don't need to fit into anyone else's category. That's the magic of authenticity—it's yours, and yours alone.

The formula for authentic confidence is simple, and it boils down to three key questions:

1. **Are you committed?**
   Are you fully invested in your mission, your goal, and the impact you want to make? Confidence is born from commitment. It's the willingness to keep showing up, even when it's hard.

2. **Do you know what you're talking about?**
   Have you done the work, learned, been a student, and are you continuing to learn? Confidence isn't about pretending to know everything; it's about knowing your craft well enough to teach and guide others from a place of integrity.

3. **Does it benefit all of mankind?**
   Does your work, your mission, or your message contribute to the greater good? True confidence comes from knowing that what you're doing is not just about you—it's about creating something that elevates everyone.

If the answer to these questions is yes, then congratulations—you've found your confidence. Confidence doesn't come from your appearance, your credentials, or your circumstances. It comes from within, from being so aligned with your mission that doubt doesn't stand a chance.

So, to anyone out there waiting for the perfect moment, let me tell you: it's already here. You don't need to look the part; you need to be the part. Authentic confidence is about walking into the room as yourself, not as who you think others want you to be. It's about saying, *"This is me, and this is what I have to offer."*

Your authentic spirit is your power. When you embrace it fully, you not only build your confidence—you inspire others to do the same.

Activation for Code Three: Ownership and Perspective Shifts

This code invited you to claim ownership of your perspective and approach to life. In Code Three, you're encouraged to hold space for compassion, both for yourself and others, while transcending the need for control.

Affirmations for Code Three:

- I own my perspective, recognizing its power to shape my life.

- Compassion flows from me freely, creating deeper connections with myself and others.

- I release the need for control and trust in the unfolding of life.

Prompt to Reflect: Consider, Where am I still holding on, trying to control what's meant to unfold naturally? Explore what would happen if you allowed grace to guide those parts of your life.

CODE FOUR

- Sacred Heart -

The Ripple Effect

Self-actualization is the art of becoming the masterpiece you were always meant to create.

Through the attainment of self-actualization and the healing of the heart chakra, we step into a way of life led by love. Embodying our passion and joy, we expand our capacity for kindness, empathy, and acceptance, achieving a profound peace within ourselves that ripples outward to embrace the world.

The Origin of Consciousness is in the Heart

If humanity were ever to face an intergalactic war, our greatest strength and key to triumph wouldn't be found in advanced weaponry or tactical prowess, but in something far more profound and uniquely human: our capacity for love. This powerful emotion, which binds individuals, communities, and societies, could very well be what sets us apart from extraterrestrial beings.

The depth and complexity of human love, exemplified in the unconditional love a mother has for her child, stand as a testament to our emotional depth. This form of love, encompassing sacrifice, empathy, and an unwavering bond, could be an enigma to evil entities who might possess superior technology but lack the emotional intricacies that define human relationships.

Love, in its most universal form, transcends mere sentimentality; it is the foundation upon which societies are built and the force that drives us to protect, nurture, and persevere against all odds. In the hypothetical scenario of an intergalactic conflict, it is conceivable that our adversaries could underestimate the power of human connection and the lengths to which we would go to safeguard our loved ones and our home.

This intrinsic superpower—our ability to love—serves not only as a weapon in the face of conflict but as a vital force that ensures our survival and propels our civilization forward. Through love, we find the motivation to innovate, explore, and overcome challenges. It fuels our compassion, enabling us to form alliances and work collectively towards common goals, even in the face of seemingly insurmountable obstacles.

In essence, if faced with a challenge as monumental as an intergalactic war, it would be our heart's capacity to love that would unify humanity, inspiring acts of heroism, sacrifice, and solidarity. This profound ability to love, deeply ingrained in our very being, could ultimately be what ensures not just our survival but our triumph. Hate to be cheesy but love truly is the answer.

The Power of Forgiveness: A Journey to Healing the Heart

Forgiveness is often misunderstood as forgetting or excusing the wrongs done to us. However, true forgiveness is a profound act of the heart, an essential step on our journey of self-discovery and healing. It's about recognizing the humanity in ourselves and others, understanding that we are all travelers on this earth, each facing our own jungles of lessons.

Just as we discussed the importance of seeing our parents as fellow humans walking this earth journey with us, forgiveness begins with this same realization. Our parents, like us, are imperfect beings, doing their best with the tools and knowledge they have. By seeing them through this lens, we start to dismantle the pedestal of expectations and allow room for compassion. This shift in perspective is the first step toward forgiveness.

Forgiveness is not about erasing memories or condoning actions; it's the heart's way of releasing the heavy burdens that hinder our growth. When we forgive, we free ourselves from the chains of resentment and anger, creating space for love and joy to flourish. This process begins within. We must first learn to forgive ourselves for our own perceived shortcomings and mistakes.

Forgive yourself for all the times you abandoned your heart and looked for love outside yourself.

You will never truly be able to forgive others until you have learned to forgive yourself. Self-forgiveness involves acknowledging our humanity, accepting our flaws, and embracing our journey with kindness. It is about understanding that making mistakes is a part of being human and that each error is a lesson leading us toward greater wisdom and self-awareness.

The journey to forgiveness is a journey to healing the heart. It involves accepting that everyone, including ourselves, is imperfect, cultivating compassion for ourselves and others, letting go of grudges and resentments that weigh us down, and embracing the lessons learned from each experience of hurt and betrayal.

Forgiveness is a gift we give ourselves. It's a way to cleanse the heart, allowing us to move forward with a lighter spirit and a deeper understanding of love and compassion. By embarking on this journey, we not only heal our hearts but also create a ripple effect of peace and kindness in the world around us.

Vibrating with abundance means embracing life fully and recognizing that true wealth comes from our experiences, not material possessions. It's found in the simplicity of each breath, the beauty of each sunrise, and the warmth of every smile. This abundance goes beyond financial gain and is a daily practice of generosity, gratitude, and celebrating life's treasures.

To master yourself and simplify your journey, consider the wisdom of old ways, where harmony with nature was key. Simplification starts with acknowledging the basic need for happiness and approaching life with a lightness of being.

Part of this is learning to forgive easily, which becomes more accessible through open communication and admitting our mistakes. Our ability to extend grace and compassion to others reflects how we treat ourselves.

Avoid turning small issues into big challenges. Reflect on teachings that remind us not to let unfounded fears cloud our vision. Create a list of what truly matters in your life—love, family, financial well-being—and assess these areas honestly. This grounds your journey, ensuring you move forward with clarity and purpose.

Understanding yourself is the cornerstone of making life easier. Be genuine, not an imposter wearing a mask. When your actions reflect your true self, life flows more naturally. Embrace all parts of yourself and commit to personal growth. This self-acceptance and dedication prevent you from living as someone else and empower you to walk your path authentically.

Living true to ourselves and our purpose helps life's complexities unravel, revealing a path where our actions, passions, and truths align. This is the essence of a life vibrating with abundance, rooted in self-knowledge and authenticity, celebrated through simple, profound joys. Embrace all of yourself and work on what needs improvement. This helps you avoid living someone else's life as an imposter.

The extent to which you love yourself is the extent to which you can love others. And let's be honest—no one dishes out the harshness to our hearts quite like we do. We're our own worst critics, holding onto every little mistake, every moment we've let ourselves down. We carry those moments around like heavy baggage, always there, always reminding us of where we went wrong. But here's the kicker—before we can truly forgive others, we need to clear the path to forgiving the person who often needs it the most: ourselves.

Think back to when you were a child, playing with friends under the open sky. Where have those friends gone? Without realizing it, there came a day when you all played together for the last time. It wasn't planned, and it wasn't personal—just life doing what it does, moving us from one phase to another. It was a natural part of growing up, moving away from each other without any hard feelings, simply a transition that moved your circle further and further away. When you think of their faces and laughs, does your heart expand? Now think of your circle of friends in high school, college, and more recent years. It's a little different, isn't it? As our ego develops, our resentment grows with it, creating barriers of plaque around our hearts.

Holding onto resentment and setting unrealistic expectations for others only serves to imprison our spirits in a cycle of negativity. We think we're protecting ourselves by building those walls, but in reality, we're just trapping ourselves in with our own bitterness. Letting go isn't just about freeing others from our judgment; it's about liberating ourselves from the prison of bitterness. When we make space in our hearts by forgiving others, we create the room necessary to forgive the person we often treat the worst—ourselves.

If there's a particular relationship in your life that leaves you feeling uneasy, consider offering prayers not only for those close to you but also for yourself. Praying for both friends and those who have hurt us fosters a spirit of forgiveness and understanding. It's not about pretending the hurt didn't happen or that it didn't matter. It's about recognizing that holding onto that hurt only serves to deepen the wounds. When you pray for others, and for yourself, you're not just asking for healing—you're creating it. It cleanses our hearts, freeing us from the burdens of animosity and allowing us to embrace the love and admiration that await on the other side.

Remember, our capacity to love and forgive isn't measured by the wrongs done to us but by the love we extend despite them. In healing our hearts and letting go of past grievances, we open ourselves to a world of love and self-acceptance. Misunderstandings, disagreements—they're just part of being human. They don't define us, and they don't have to dictate our future. Forgiveness is about tuning into a higher frequency where love and understanding reign supreme.

Sometimes, people drift apart, not because of some epic fallout, but because they're vibing on a different frequency. It's like trying to listen to jazz on a rock station—it just doesn't work. But instead of forcing it, what if you just let it be? Giving space, allowing time for both of you to grow, is an act of love. Not just for them, but for you too. Who knows? Maybe one day, you'll find that your frequencies align again, stronger than before. And if they don't? That's okay too. Not every relationship is meant to last forever. Some are just meant to teach us something, and then move on.

So, forgive others, but most importantly, forgive yourself. Stop being so hard on yourself. Cut the ties to the grudges weighing you down, and let your heart breathe a little easier. Because when you make room for forgiveness, you make room for a better, lighter version of yourself—one that's ready to move forward without all the baggage. And isn't that what we all want? To move forward, free from the past, and open to whatever comes next.

Finding Your Passion

Be Passionate About Everything Instead of finding that one thing you are passionate about, ask yourself, "Why aren't I passionate about everything I do?" Be passionate about everything you're currently doing. Flow with them.

Run With What You Love Lean into what sets your soul on fire. When I talk about following your path, it's a bit of a curveball. Turns out, getting really good at something you weren't initially into can be super rewarding. We're all about chasing our passions, right? But what happens when that passion starts to feel a bit meh? That's when you gotta find that thing—that spark that really makes you feel alive—and go all in.

Listen to your gut and excel at what truly makes you tick. The stuff that makes you forget time? Think about what makes you genuinely happy, even if there's no paycheck attached.

For me, photography was cool until it wasn't. But creating for House of Vibration? That's where I hit my stride, getting lost in creating and sharing stuff that matters.

Sticking to this path isn't always smooth sailing. It's not about being 100% passionate 24/7 or dodging tough days. It's about pouring your heart and soul into what you believe in, making sure everything you do reflects who you are and what you stand for. It's living a life that's true to you, filled with purpose and passion, and connecting deeply with what you do. That's how you honor your true self and craft the legacy you dream of.

In our journey through life, each of us walks a unique path, marked by the gifts and responsibilities bestowed upon us. Like the diverse roles within a tribe, where every member contributes to the well-being of the community, our society thrives on the varied strengths and talents of its people. Reflecting on the roles we play among our families, friends, and colleagues can illuminate our purpose and reveal the gifts we have to offer.

Consider the structure of a tribe, where each role, from the healer to the storyteller, the hunter to the craftsman, is vital. The healer brings physical and spiritual wellness, the storyteller preserves our records and lessons, the hunter provides nourishment, and the craftsman creates tools and art for daily life. Each role, while distinct, is interconnected, ensuring the community's survival and prosperity.

In modern terms, finding your niche means recognizing your unique contributions—whether you're the innovator, the mediator, the nurturer, or the explorer. It's about understanding that your passion is a powerful tool for fulfilling your purpose. This doesn't mean striving to be the best in every field but nurturing your innate talents and using them to serve others.

Facing challenges or feeling lost can often lead to a deeper understanding of our path. If you're uncertain about your direction, commit wholeheartedly to your pursuits. With time and dedication, your true calling will become clear. Remember, the essence of our journey is not just in achieving personal success but in how we contribute to the well-being of others.

Embrace the wisdom of living in harmony with our community and the Earth. Recognize your strengths, nurture your passions, and use them to enrich the lives of those around you. By aligning our actions with the greater good, we honor the interconnectedness of all life and contribute to a world where every individual has the opportunity to thrive. This alignment with our inner being and the roles we play in our communities forms the foundation of a fulfilling life, woven from the threads of individual purpose and collective harmony.

Like my beautiful soulmate once said to me, my passion is just a tool for my purpose.

If you don't know your purpose in life simply pressure yourself, becoming the healthiest, most blissful, healed, forgiving, present, assertive version of your highest self, it will reveal itself.

"If you choose something and you put your heart and soul into it, it's bound to be great. I promise you. Get started with any part of it; it starts with simply putting it on paper. You'll never feel truly ready, I promise you. You'll never have the money, the time, the support, and the talent enough to feel 100% ready. I remember my old boss sat me down one day and said, 'Natalie, I know it seems like we're the only company in the world who is just making things up as we go, but I'm friends with the Walmarts and big CEOs of the world and you know what we do? We laugh about the fact that we have no clue what the fuck we're doing.' This came from a man worth 1.2 billion, but it still made me upset."

As a kid, I was convinced I'd follow in the footsteps of my favorite aunt and become a dentist. The pristine clinics, the promise of bright smiles—it all seemed perfect until I witnessed the behind-the-scenes of a root canal. The blood and aroma of the client's breath were enough to make me faint, and just like that, my dental dreams dissolved.

For a long while afterward, I wandered, unsure of my true calling. Yet, even amidst this uncertainty, I held onto one clear truth: to excel in whatever task lay before me. I may not have known my destination, but I was determined that each step, each endeavor, would be a stride toward excellence. It was my way of embracing life, trusting that in this rich journey, my purpose would reveal itself. If that meant I was hired to clean someone's floor, I promised to be the best damn floor cleaner the world had ever seen.

Consider the quest for purpose as opening your heart, allowing not just others in but giving yourself the chance to explore and grow. It's like the well-meaning advice in dating, "Give them a chance." It's not just about the other person; it's about allowing yourself to discover and connect.

Your purpose intertwines with your aspirations. We often hear goals like wanting happiness and health, noble yet broad targets if you ask me. Your purpose, however, is precise, a beacon shaped by visions and expressed with heartfelt sincerity. It's your unique contribution to humanity's grand tapestry, a piece in the puzzle of collective existence, significant no matter how modest it may seem.

So, at 29, I realized I had a choice in how I viewed my past. I could lament the years spent searching, or I could celebrate every moment lived with zeal and passion. I chose the latter, embracing the belief that my journey, each part of it, was a chapter of a life lived fully and passionately. And with that realization, my journey towards my true passion began.

If you don't know what your passion is, ask yourself, "Instead of being passionate about one thing, why am I not passionate about all things?"

Making it Look Easy

While in Japan, I was fascinated by how effortlessly everything seemed perfect. Their self-presentation, poise, cleanliness, manners, and speech were all impressive. The most remarkable thing was how they made everything look so easy, seamless, and graceful. Watching them, I wondered, "How do they do that and make it look so easy?"

Sometimes, you look at people like I used to look at my mom. Every time she ate potato chips, her fingers never got dirty, while mine were always stained. She made everything look so tasteful. Now, as I grow older, I try to do the same things and realize, "This is way harder than it looked."

This realization led me to understand that true mastery comes from within. My dad worked in hospitality as a waiter for over 30 years. He balanced heavy trays, interacted with people, and remained the most graceful person in the room. Growing up, I worked various jobs, including as a waitress, despite my father's warnings. I thought if he did it for many years, how hard could it be? Newsflash: I was a mess. I got orders wrong, dropped plates, and hated the smell of food on me. I couldn't figure out how my dad and others made it look so graceful while I constantly looked like a mess.

I love seeing true masters in their space, like my partner, a cinematographer, who exhibits grace in every image and set. He can put anyone at ease and commands control in the chillest way possible.

Have you ever been served by a waiter who makes you feel like not ordering again? The best waiters come from those who have mastered themselves. It's like when you get your nails done—you want to be comfortable with the person attending to you. It's the same in sales; you want to make the client feel relaxed and stress-free.

So, how do we give off that energy? Passion is key. If you want to pursue a career or craft, you must first master yourself. How do you come off to others? Social cues are important. Be aware of when you are or aren't doing things properly. Mastering yourself means knowing your audience and when to stop talking.

"Simplicity is the most complicated thing to master."

Love as the Ultimate Currency

Understanding the human heart as our biggest gift reveals its true purpose: it is the highway through which our soul flows into the physical world. From the heart, we experience compassion, connection, and the ability to truly *feel* for one another. The heart isn't just a pump for life; it's the center of our power, the source of our ability to give and receive, to love and create.

I remember working in corporate, where every few months, a new character would join the mix. Without fail, they came with the same story—a savior of sorts who was supposed to fix all the company's problems, accelerate growth, unite teams, and fulfill the vision. But even in the corporate world, my intuitive senses refused to switch off. One of my bosses, who trusted my gut more than any policy or resume, often confided in me and asked for my insights on these new recruits, even when they were higher-ups. Without fail, I was always right about them.

She'd ask me, *"How do you know?"* and all I could say was, *"I feel it."* But that word—*feel*—was a trigger for her. In the world of corporate structure, where decisions are supposed to come from logic, data, and metrics, *feeling* is seen as the enemy.

That's when I realized just how much this world tries to block our natural highway to bliss. We're told that to feel deeply is a weakness, that softness is vulnerability, and vulnerability is a liability. But the truth is, *to feel is to be powerful.* To be soft is to be unshakable.

Look at the most extraordinary people in your life—the ones who are always there for you, the ones who hold space, who give endlessly, who love without conditions. So many of them are natural nurturers, the people-pleasers who've been hurt time and again. After heartbreak, betrayal, or abuse, they often feel forced to shut down their superpower—their heart—and transform into what they think the world expects: something harder, colder, less giving.

I get it. When the world takes and takes, when kindness is mistaken for weakness, it can feel like the only way to survive is to block yourself off completely. But here's the truth: the lesson is never about becoming hard. It's about learning your boundaries while keeping your heart open. Because the moment you let the world make you hard, you cut yourself off from your greatest gift.

The heart is the source of the ultimate currency—love. And this currency doesn't just flow in one direction. It's a cycle, a constant exchange that works physically, spiritually, and emotionally. Love is what sustains us, what fuels us, what allows us to create, grow, and thrive.

When we block ourselves off—when we stop loving, stop giving, and stop *feeling*—we sever that flow. The currency dries up. But when we keep our hearts open, when we stay loving and true despite the trials of the world, we create abundance. Love is magnetic. It attracts kindness, opportunities, and healing in ways no material wealth can match.

In corporate, I often watched my predictions about people play out. Those who operated from a place of fear, ego, and power-hunger always hit walls. They could manipulate for a while, but their energy would eventually ripple out, creating mistrust and disconnection. On the other hand, those who led with heart, who cared deeply for their teams, created an energy that couldn't be faked. Their success wasn't just in numbers—it was in the way people rallied behind them, inspired and connected.

The world will try to teach you that being cold, calculated, and "strong" is the way forward. But true strength lies in staying open, soft, and in tune with your heart. This doesn't mean being a doormat or letting people take advantage of you. It means knowing your boundaries, speaking your truth, and giving love freely without expecting anything in return.

Never let the world make you hard. Stay loving. Stay true. This is how we allow the ultimate currency—love—to flow through every aspect of our lives, creating abundance not just for ourselves but for everyone we touch.

Because love, when exchanged authentically, isn't just a gift. It's the most valuable form of energy we have.

The Sacred Exchange

When we talk about money, it's crucial to recognize that it's not just about currency—it's energy, a flow that connects people, ideas, and intentions across the world. Money is profoundly spiritual because it's tied to your intentions, your purpose, and your mission in life. It's a physical representation of the value you create in the world and the abundance you are open to receiving. When you see money as spiritual, you begin to understand that it's not just about wealth; it's about the energy you put into earning, spending, and sharing it.

But many of us have a toxic relationship with money, one that often stems from a deep place of inner worth and trust, or rather, the lack thereof. We're subconsciously programmed to believe that we're not worthy of abundance, that money is somehow tainted, or that it will corrupt us. We might even think that if we had money, we wouldn't use it wisely, or worse, that it would change us for the worse. These beliefs are deeply rooted in self-doubt and can create a cycle of scarcity and fear, where we either push money away or cling to it too tightly, afraid that we'll never have enough.

This programming convinces us that financial abundance is incompatible with spiritual integrity or a good heart. But this is a lie. The belief that we wouldn't be capable of doing good on this planet if we had money is a reflection of our inner struggles with self-worth and trust in ourselves. When we doubt our ability to manage money or fear it will change us, we're really doubting our capacity to stay true to our values and purpose.

Allowing yourself to earn and generate wealth is one of the most selfless, yet profoundly self-loving, acts you can engage in. It's a declaration to the universe that you love yourself so much that you refuse to sit idly by, complaining about the world's problems. Instead, you choose to go out there, produce, and contribute to the solutions. When people say that money doesn't make them happy, they're often lying or haven't truly experienced what financial freedom can offer. Science backs this up—money does impact happiness, not because it buys superficial pleasures, but because it enables you to fulfill the mission God sent you here to master.

There's a lot wrong in the world, and while money alone can't fix everything, it sure helps. It's not about supporting ridiculous lifestyles; it's about fueling the mission and purpose you were born to achieve. Money, in this context, is not just currency—it's a sacred exchange of energy, respect, and value.

For energy workers, therapists, coaches, leaders, or teachers, anyone who is here on this planet serving others, this understanding is vital. The act of giving and receiving in financial terms is a sacred transaction that honors the spiritual work being done. When clients invest financially in their healing journey, they are energetically committing to their own growth, making the transformation deeper and more lasting. Investing in yourself is a powerful act of self-care, setting off a cycle of abundance and well-being. Charging for your work ensures you have the resources to maintain your energy and impact others effectively.

Negotiating big deals or making decisions around money shouldn't be about winning or losing; it's about alignment and ensuring that both parties are walking away feeling fulfilled and respected. This is where the heart-centered approach comes in. When entering negotiations, especially for significant deals, it's crucial to stay connected to your heart and your higher purpose. Ask yourself: How can this deal serve the greater good? How can it align with my mission and values?

Allow yourself to be used by God in these moments. When you approach negotiations from a place of love and service, you open the door for divine guidance. It's not just about getting the best financial outcome; it's about creating an agreement that resonates with your soul's purpose. When your heart is centered, and your intentions are pure, the negotiation process becomes a spiritual practice. You're not just working for yourself; you're working as an instrument of God, allowing divine energy to flow through you to create outcomes that benefit all involved.

Healing your relationship with money requires recognizing that it's not just a tool but a reflection of what you cultivate inside. By aligning your financial actions with your spiritual beliefs and trusting in your ability to do good, you can transform money from a source of stress and toxicity into a powerful ally in your journey to fulfill your purpose on this planet. Remember, money is made from a soul. It's not just a necessity but a sacred resource that helps you achieve your highest potential and contribute to the greater good.

Feeling good—being healthy in both mind and body—plays a crucial role in attracting money and abundance into your life. When you're in a state of well-being, your energy is vibrant, your mind is clear, and your heart is open. This alignment allows you to operate at your highest frequency, making it easier to draw in the opportunities, people, and resources that contribute to financial success.

Think of it this way: when you're healthy, you radiate positivity and confidence. This energy is magnetic, attracting like-minded individuals and situations that align with your goals. People are naturally drawn to those who exude vitality and enthusiasm because it signals that you're capable, trustworthy, and ready to handle whatever comes your way. Your physical and mental health becomes a beacon, guiding prosperity toward you.

Moreover, when your mind and body are in harmony, you're better equipped to make sound decisions. A clear mind can see opportunities where others see obstacles, and a healthy body provides the stamina needed to pursue those opportunities with vigor. You're more resilient in the face of challenges and more creative in finding solutions. This combination of mental clarity and physical vitality creates a fertile ground for financial growth.

In contrast, when you're not feeling your best—whether due to stress, poor health, or negative emotions—your energy is low, and your focus is scattered. This state of being can block the flow of abundance, making it harder to attract the wealth and success you desire. Your thoughts may become clouded by doubt and fear, leading to missed opportunities or decisions that don't serve your highest good.

At its core, money is energy, and it flows more freely when you're aligned with your true self—when you're feeling good, healthy, and balanced. By prioritizing your well-being, you're not just taking care of yourself; you're also cultivating the optimal conditions for attracting wealth and abundance into your life. When you feel good, you're naturally more open to receiving, more capable of handling success, and more attuned to the opportunities that will lead you to greater financial freedom

The Loudest Way to Love

Making someone feel seen, heard, and understood is the loudest way to love them. It's about tuning into their frequency, meeting them where they are, and riding the vibrational wave alongside them. When you truly connect with someone on this level, it's like you're telling them, "I get you. I'm here with you." This isn't just about empathy; it's about creating a safe space where they can be their authentic selves without fear of judgment or rejection. It's a powerful act of love that resonates deeply, often more than words ever could.

But life has a way of testing us, especially when it comes to those who have caused us pain. There will be moments when someone you care about is going through something so heavy, so deeply personal, that you can't even begin to comprehend it. Maybe it's the death of a loved one, a battle with depression, the loss of a job, or a breakup that's tearing them apart. These are the times when you might feel completely out of your depth, unsure of how to show up for them because you've never walked in their shoes.

We've all been there—frozen in uncertainty, unsure of what to say or do. It's easy to drift away, not out of a lack of care, but because we can't find the right words. We don't want to say the wrong thing, so we say nothing at all, and before we know it, the distance has grown. But the truth is, in those moments, it's not about finding the perfect words or having all the answers. It's about simply being there, riding the wave with them, and letting them know they're not alone.

Take, for example, a situation that comes up often when someone loses a loved one. You might hear people say, "I didn't write to them because I didn't even know what to say." But here's the thing—your words, no matter how imperfect, are special because you took the time to reach out. The act of writing, even when you don't know what to say, is what makes it meaningful. It's your way of saying, "I'm here. I care. You're not going through this alone."

And then, there will come a day when you'll have the opportunity to see someone who hurt you at their lowest point.

This moment will challenge you in ways you may not expect, presenting you with three options: to spit on them, to observe and ignore, or to lift them to your highest point.

When this happens, it's a test of your own growth and humanity. The easiest path might be to spit on them, to return the pain they once caused you. It's the knee-jerk reaction, the one that feels justified in the moment. But what does it really achieve? It only perpetuates the cycle of pain and resentment, keeping you both locked in a negative spiral.

The second option, to observe and ignore, may feel like the neutral choice—neither helping nor hurting. It's the decision to stand back and let karma do its thing, believing that you're rising above by not engaging. But in reality, this choice often leaves unresolved energy hanging in the air, a tension that neither heals nor grows.

The third option, and the most challenging, is to lift them to your highest point. To offer them kindness, compassion, and understanding, even when you might feel they do not deserve it. This isn't about condoning what they did or forgetting the hurt they caused. It's about choosing to rise above, to break the cycle, and to show them, and yourself, that you're capable of love that transcends past wounds.

When you choose this path, you're not just helping them— you're healing yourself. You're releasing the grip that pain has on your heart and freeing up space for something greater. In that moment, you become a beacon of what it truly means to be human, to be compassionate, to be love in action.

So when that day comes, and you're faced with that choice, remember that the most powerful act of love isn't always easy, but it's the one that will elevate both you and the person in need. Ride that vibrational wave, not just with those you love, but even with those who've hurt you. Because in the end, how you respond in those moments is what defines your journey and the kind of energy you bring into the world.

Never a Waste

One of the most profound truths about walking this earth is that we are all just *walking each other home*. Some journeys last a lifetime, while others are fleeting—a shared laugh, a moment of connection, or a season of growth. But no matter the length, the act of love is never wasted.

I often hear people vent about how someone they dated was their "biggest mistake." They'll lament, *"I wasted so much time on them,"* as if their love was poured into a void, as if their effort, energy, and heart weren't worth it because the outcome didn't meet their expectations. But here's the thing: your love is never wasted.

There's no such thing as someone **wasting your time**. Every connection—whether in a business deal, a friendship, a romantic partnership, or even a passing interaction—has its purpose. Our partnerships are some of our greatest teachers. And just as they teach us, we are also their mirrors, reflecting lessons, growth, and, yes, sometimes the hard truths we may not want to see.

Love is not a transaction. It's not about giving and receiving in perfect balance, measuring out who loves more or less, or pulling back because the scales feel uneven. Love is an act of divine expression. It flows freely when it's authentic, without expectation or attachment to how it will be received.

When you withhold love because you feel it isn't being equally returned, you're not protecting yourself—you're stepping into the role of playing God, trying to determine what someone "deserves." But love is not about deserving. It's about giving. Love given freely is a gift, not a gamble. The reward isn't in the outcome; it's in the act itself.

Think about it: the love you pour into someone doesn't disappear just because the relationship ends. That love becomes part of their story, part of their healing, part of their growth. And it becomes part of yours, too. It's not about whether they loved you back in the same way or whether they stayed in your life. It's about how that love shaped you, expanded you, and allowed you to grow into a deeper understanding of yourself.

Pulling back because you feel someone loves you less is a misunderstanding of love's power. Love isn't a finite resource—it's infinite. The more you give, the more it flows. That doesn't mean you allow yourself to be mistreated or undervalued; boundaries are essential. But love, when given from a place of authenticity, never diminishes—it only strengthens.

So stop questioning whether you've given too much. Stop playing the role of judge and jury over who deserves your love. The answer is always yes. Yes, they deserved it because they taught you something, even if that lesson came through pain. Yes, you deserved to give it, because in doing so, you stepped into your most divine, human essence.

Even the heartbreaks, the ones that leave us gutted, are part of this journey of walking each other home. Those moments remind us of the beauty of connection, the vulnerability of love, and the strength it takes to keep our hearts open.

The next time you're tempted to call someone your "biggest mistake," pause. Reflect on what they taught you. Maybe they taught you about boundaries. Maybe they taught you about the kind of love you no longer want. Maybe they taught you that you're capable of loving deeply, even when it feels scary.

Love isn't something to be tallied, measured, or rationed. It's meant to flow through you, to expand, to teach, and to heal. Your love was never wasted, and it never will be. So walk with others for as long as the journey allows, and when the paths diverge, let your heart be grateful for the time you shared.

Because at the end of the day, love is not about how it's received—it's about how freely it's given.

"Everything I lose creates space for everything I need"

In Order to Master Your Craft, One Must Learn to Master Oneself

Mastering your craft begins with mastering yourself. This means understanding your strengths and weaknesses, knowing your true desires, and being honest with yourself. Self-mastery involves continuous self-improvement, self-discipline, and self-awareness. Here are some key aspects:

1. **Self-Discipline:** To become proficient in any craft, you must develop self-discipline. This includes setting goals, creating a plan, and sticking to it, even when it's difficult. Self-discipline helps you stay focused and committed to your craft.

2. **Self-Awareness:** Understanding your emotions, triggers, and reactions is crucial. Self-awareness allows you to manage your emotions effectively, leading to better decision-making and interactions with others. It helps you identify areas for improvement and recognize your progress.

3. **Self-Reflection:** Regular self-reflection helps you evaluate your actions and their impact. It enables you to learn from your experiences and make necessary adjustments. Reflecting on your successes and failures fosters growth and resilience.

4. **Embracing Vulnerability:** Mastering yourself requires embracing your vulnerabilities. Acknowledge your fears and insecurities, and use them as opportunities for growth. Vulnerability fosters authenticity and deeper connections with others.

5. **Continuous Learning:** Stay curious and open to learning. Seek knowledge and experiences that challenge you and expand your skills. Continuous learning keeps you adaptable and innovative in your craft.

6. **Mindfulness and Presence:** Practice mindfulness to stay present and focused. Being fully engaged in the moment enhances your performance and creativity. Mindfulness helps you manage stress and maintain a balanced perspective.

Activation Code Four

In this code, we explored the journey of self-actualization through the deep strength and power in open hearted living. Central to this journey is the realisation that self-actualization is about becoming the masterpiece we were always meant to create. By healing the resistance we have to vulnerability, we open ourselves to a way of life led by love, embodying our passion and joy while expanding our capacity for kindness, empathy, and acceptance. Through various reflections and exercises, we uncovered the importance of embracing our passions, forgiving ourselves for past abandonments of the heart, and reconnecting with the wisdom of our inner child. Additionally, we delved into mastering ourselves and simplifying our journey, recognizing the abundance within and aligning our actions with our true purpose. Finally, we explored the miracle of life itself, acknowledging the lessons present in every moment and embracing the cyclical nature of existence.

Affirmations For Integrating Code Four

- "I open my heart to love and compassion, embracing the journey of self-actualization with grace and courage."

- "I forgive myself for past betrayals of the heart, releasing any guilt or shame that weighs me down."

- "I reconnect with the wisdom of my inner child, honoring my true passions and desires."

- "I align my actions with my true purpose, living a life filled with authenticity, meaning, and fulfillment."

- "I embrace the abundance within and around me, recognizing that true wealth lies in the richness of experiences and connections."

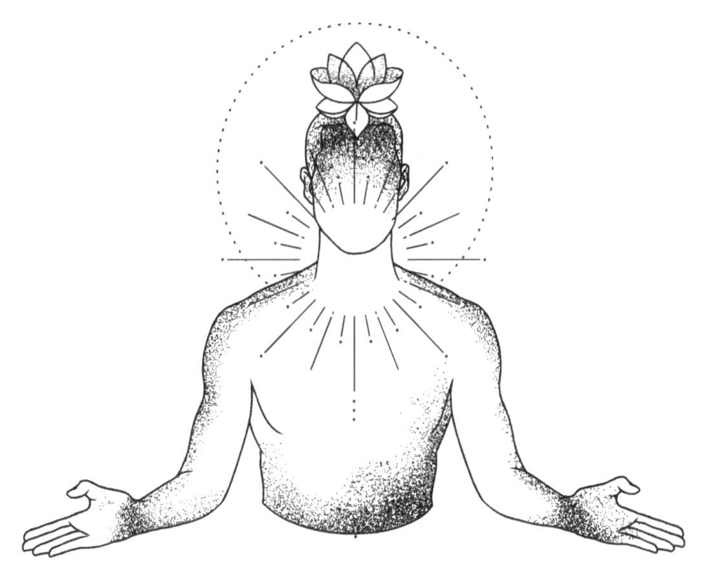

CODE FIVE

- The First Language -

As we move through the intricate dance of human connections, the throat chakra acts as the compass, guiding us towards the authentic expression of our innermost selves.

Healing this energetic center amplifies our capacity for sincere communication, honesty, and pure, genuine self-expression is elevated, transforming our interactions with the external world into bridges that connect hearts and souls.

Do Prophets Still Exist?

Have you ever been at a loss for words in a moment that demanded the perfect thing to say? Those tough situations—when the weight of the moment feels almost too heavy to bear—are where the essence of Code Five comes into play. It's about always finding the right words, not because you've rehearsed or calculated them, but because they flow from a place of alignment, courage, and truth.

When you walk with integrity and good intentions, you can't go wrong with your words. They become more than just sounds or phrases—they turn into vessels for impact, connection, and truth. Code Five isn't just about communication; it's about embodiment. When you're true to yourself, the words follow naturally.

Here's the thing: words are just the surface. What truly matters is the energy behind them. It's not just about what you say—it's about what you stand for. When you're aligned with your purpose and deeply connected to something greater than yourself, the clarity you need is always available. Even in the most challenging conversations, you find yourself guided to speak with confidence and truth, as if the universe itself is lending you the perfect language.

Let's take it deeper. Speech, the ability to communicate, is one of the most divine gifts the Great Spirit has given us. It's not just about exchanging information; it's a tool for connection, inspiration, and transformation. Through words, we have the power to heal, to teach, and to transcend the physical.

When people talk about receiving "downloads" or invoking "the word," they're describing a spiritual connection—a moment when divine wisdom flows directly through them. It's not about having the most degrees or the biggest vocabulary; it's about being open. It's about tuning into that higher frequency and letting the message come through. This isn't some mystical mumbo jumbo; it's the way pastors, spiritual leaders, and even everyday people connect with their source. They're tapping into divine inspiration that flows straight into the crown chakra, downloading insight and energy directly into their being.

Take speaking in tongues, for example. As a kid, I'd visit friends' churches and watch people speaking in tongues, utterly terrified because I had no idea what was happening. No one explained that it's essentially spiritual freestyling—a raw, unfiltered connection to the divine. Now that I get it, I realize how amazing it actually is. It's not exclusive to Pentecostal Christians either; variations of this phenomenon show up in cultures and religions worldwide. It's a universal expression of humanity's deep desire to connect with something greater.

Whether skeptics dismiss it as psychological or cultural, speaking in tongues—and other forms of divine communication—points to something profound. Studies have shown that during these moments, the brain's control centers quiet down, indicating a unique state of consciousness. Call it divine guidance or an altered state of mind—either way, it's a testament to how deeply humans crave connection with the ineffable.

And let's not stop there. Divine communication isn't limited to church pews or spiritual ceremonies. It's something you can access in everyday life. Whether you're negotiating a business deal or mending a strained relationship, staying open to divine guidance can transform your words into something profound. When you align with your source, you're no longer just speaking—you're channeling wisdom, healing, and clarity.

The fear of misspeaking often holds us back. But here's the secret: when you approach your conversations with pure intention and a connection to your higher self, there's no "right" or "wrong." The words will flow exactly as they're meant to, carrying the energy that's needed in the moment. It's not about perfection; it's about being a vessel for the truth.

So, do prophets still exist? Absolutely. A prophet isn't someone standing on a mountaintop with lightning bolts in their hands. A prophet is anyone who dares to speak from their soul, aligned with their truth, and connected to a higher purpose. It's the person who takes a deep breath, centers themselves, and says what needs to be said—not to impress, but to inspire.

This divine aspect of communication is a reminder that when we open ourselves to the wisdom of the universe, we unlock a power far beyond what we thought possible. Our words become more than just tools—they become bridges. Bridges that connect us to each other, to our source, and to the infinite potential of love, healing, and transformation.

"You can tell someone a thousand words but most can only hear you vibrationally."

Maintaining Me and You

From the bonds of love and companionship to the ties we hold with friends, colleagues, and most importantly, ourselves, every relationship reflects aspects of who we are. How we show up for others mirrors our inner essence, and the energy we cast outward becomes the energy we attract back.

At the core of any great relationship—be it romantic, platonic, or professional—is friendship. Friendship is the foundation, the soil where deeper connections take root. Think of the most beautiful lovebirds you've ever seen, the way they laugh, the way their eyes lock, as if they're speaking a language only they understand. Witnessing love like that feels like witnessing divinity—a reminder of the Creator's masterpiece.

This kind of connection begins with treating every person as a companion on the journey, even when disagreements arise. It's in those moments, when storms threaten to shake us, that extending the simple grace of friendship becomes the deepest form of respect. True connection is about walking through the hard times with compassion and understanding, not just enjoying the easy moments.

But maintaining this kind of connection requires effort. It requires choosing to rise above fleeting irritations and choosing grace over being right. Strength lies in the courage to untangle knots of misunderstanding, to meet the moment with a willingness to listen, and to create a space where respect deepens and trust grows.

Even in the heat of conflict, humanity should remain at the forefront. If arguments with a parent, partner, or friend seem to replay on a loop, ask yourself: "Do I truly know them? Have I tried to understand their perspective?" It's a humbling exercise to step outside your role—whether as a child, partner, or friend—and see the person in front of you as an equal, as someone with their own struggles and stories. Only then can real healing and connection begin.

This principle extends inward. Too often, we are harsh with ourselves in ways we'd never be with those we love. Taking time to pause, to treat ourselves with kindness, and to nurture the friendship we have with our inner self is foundational. It's about recognizing that we are beings of this Earth, infused with life's breath, and that we deserve the same compassion we extend to others.

A practice that has anchored me in this work is writing down the names of those I hold dear without condition. It's a simple yet powerful act of clarity—a commitment to the relationships that matter most. These are the people who receive my unconditional love, but it's also a reminder that outer-circle relationships, the ones that may feel less certain, require effort too. Friendships, like well-loved paths, need maintenance to flourish and mend when weary.

In romantic relationships, building a foundation of friendship is like nurturing a garden. Seasons change, and so do the needs and expectations of the bond. It's about adaptability, effort, and, sometimes, the wisdom to let go when the path diverges for the well-being of both souls.

Consciously choosing to show up, to initiate gatherings, and to seek understanding is a commitment not just to others but to yourself. Each conversation, each act of kindness, becomes a vessel for positivity and growth. When we embrace this way of being, we don't just elevate our own lives; we ripple that energy outward, touching others in ways we may never fully see.

And yes, sometimes letting go is part of the journey. But endings don't erase the love that once was—they mark growth, evolution, and the next steps for everyone involved. Relationships don't fail; they transform, teaching us lessons that prepare us for what's next.

This awareness also extends to the energy we bring into spaces. Every interaction is an exchange, a chance to contribute light or shadow. By reflecting on how we show up, we take responsibility for nurturing healthier, more vibrant connections. This self-awareness transforms us into people who inspire and uplift, radiating positivity wherever we go.

For example, planning a group trip is a microcosm of community dynamics. As a Virgo, I naturally fall into the role of planner. I'll map out every detail with excitement, but only if the group meets me halfway with input and support. When that doesn't happen, frustration creeps in, and I disengage. This scenario highlights how relationships thrive when we recognize and value each person's unique strengths. Maybe one friend is great at logistics, another keeps morale high, and someone else navigates unfamiliar spaces like a pro. When each role is clear and appreciated, the group moves harmoniously.

At its core, effective relationships mirror the harmony we seek with the Earth and all its inhabitants. It's about mutual respect, complementary strengths, and clear communication. Challenges aren't burdens—they're opportunities for others to step in and shine. This creates a foundation of interdependence where everyone feels valued and supported.

A mantra that grounds me in this work is: "I am a bearer of light and positivity, consciously nurturing the space around me." It's a simple yet profound reminder of the energy we bring into the world and the impact it can have.

When we approach relationships with this mindset—whether they're with friends, family, colleagues, or ourselves—we elevate every interaction. We become individuals who add value, encourage growth, and create spaces where others feel seen and supported. It's a practice that enriches not only our connections but also our lives, fostering a cycle of positivity that radiates far beyond us.

Watch Out For The Ego Trap

Sometimes, taking ourselves too seriously is just our ego puffing up like a proud peacock. But remember, even if a feather drifts away from a peacock, the bird struts on unfazed. Likewise, in the grand dance of life, if we were to suddenly vanish, the world would keep spinning. We're much like a feather on that peacock – significant in our beauty, yet the dance goes on. This isn't to downplay our worth but to add a pinch of humility to our perspective. You're not just a feather! This is a gentle nudge not to take things too personally, as that's often where we stumble.

Consider this: you might have friends, dear as sisters or brothers, yet they've never once supported any of your business endeavors. It's easy to brood over this, feeling unappreciated, especially when you've supported their ventures. But that's my ego talking, forgetting the myriad reasons they might have for their absence. They might be working late, worn out, or simply forgetful. It's rarely personal.

It's crucial to remember that people generally aren't out to get us. Despite warnings to guard our trust, I believe most of society isn't scheming against us. The person you suspect of slighting you likely hasn't spared it a second thought. Instead of stewing over perceived slights, why not consider what's on their plate? Maybe start a conversation rather than jumping to conclusions.

Next time you're in a tight spot, ask yourself: "Do I want to be in bliss, or do I want to be right?" Ponder on that, and you might find that your peace and joy outweigh any satisfaction from winning an argument.

Isn't now the time? Why the hurry? Often, the urgency we feel is the echo of unexamined beliefs, shadows of our past selves. A life review can reveal these hidden beliefs, allowing us to question their validity, understand their impact, and decide if they need to be shifted.

Boundaries are Spiritual Protections

You know those people who just seem to suck the life out of a room? The ones where, the moment they walk in, everyone else feels a little heavier, a little less vibrant? We all know someone like that. But here's the kicker—sometimes, we're that person. Yep, it happens to the best of us, especially when life and leadership start piling on the pressure.

From the time we're little, we're taught to be careful, to keep our guard up, and not to trust too easily. While that advice is meant to protect us, it often leaves us feeling isolated, cut off from the richness of life and real, meaningful connections. But what if we could tap back into that original trust we were born with? The kind that aligns us with the world and everyone in it, like a return to the Garden of Eden. That kind of trust is about believing in the inherent goodness of people and the beauty that surrounds us when we live in harmony with the earth and each other.

Being too careful can lead us to build walls that are so high, they don't just keep the bad stuff out, they also keep the good stuff from getting in. Boundaries are important, sure, but they should work more like filters—letting in the beauty of life while keeping the negativity at bay. And just like a filter, our boundaries need regular maintenance. If we don't check in on them, they can get clogged with all the wrong things.

Some of us are extremely sensitive to the vibes around us. We walk into a room and immediately feel the energy—whether it's tense, joyful, or something in between. For those of us who are sensitive, this can be both a blessing and a curse. We absorb everything like sponges, especially when it comes to the emotions of those closest to us. Personally, I feel it all—the highs, the lows, the in-betweens. I've had to learn how to navigate this sensitivity, choosing whose energy I let in and when to put up those necessary boundaries.

But here's the thing—no matter how in tune we are, we all have those moments where we're the ones casting the shadow. Maybe it's during a dinner when we're being overly critical, or in a meeting where we just can't stop complaining. Recognizing when we're bringing down the vibe is crucial.

It's not easy to shift that energy. It doesn't happen overnight. But by paying attention to the dynamics of our relationships— whether they bring us joy or stress—we start to see the impact our energy has on others and on ourselves. Recognizing when we're the ones draining the room is the first step in breaking that cycle. It's about managing our energy, seeking out positive interactions, and focusing on the light rather than the darkness. By being mindful of what we share and how we show up, we can uplift those around us, adding value to every interaction.

Energy isn't just something we encounter; it's deeply rooted in us, passed down through generations. It's like an inheritance— sometimes a gift, sometimes a burden. Ignoring the need for regular energetic maintenance is like letting a filter go without cleaning—it clogs up, and eventually, nothing good gets through. To keep our energy clear and flowing, it's essential to make checking in on our personal boundaries a regular practice. This helps us stay open to the good stuff while keeping the negativity at bay.

As leaders, our energy is contagious. Whether we're leading a business, a family, or a community, the energy we bring sets the tone for everyone else. If we're carrying around negativity, it's going to ripple out and affect those around us. But when we take the time to cleanse and realign our energy, we model something powerful—self-care and resilience. We show others that it's okay to take care of yourself, that it's necessary to maintain a positive, vibrant aura.

Regular energetic cleanses, or "limpias" as we call them, are key to this. They help us clear out the negative, stagnant energies that build up over time. These practices restore us to our natural state—one that's aligned, clear, and capable of leading with compassion and strength. Cleansing your energy isn't just about feeling good; it's about maintaining a positive aura that lifts those around you.

To keep your energy in check, especially in your relationships, try these practices:

- **Mindful Speaking:** Think before you speak—aim for words that are truthful and kind. This aligns your speech with positive energy, creating stronger connections.

- **Active Listening:** Really listen when others talk. Give them your full attention. This deepens understanding and respect in your interactions.

- **Honest Expression:** Share your thoughts and feelings openly, but do it with compassion. This brings authenticity to your relationships.

- **Daily Mantra:** Start your day with "I am a bearer of light and positivity." Set your intention to bring good vibes into every interaction.

- **Creative Outlets:** Sing, write, paint—find ways to express yourself creatively. It helps release negative energy and encourages positive exchanges.

- **Reflection:** Take time to think about how you communicate and the energy you bring into relationships. It's about self-awareness and growth.

By embracing these practices—regular boundary maintenance, clear communication, and spiritual cleansing—we not only transform our own lives but also uplift those around us. We contribute to a cycle of positivity that ripples outward, enriching our connections and deepening our alignment with the world. This journey of mindful interaction is about living fully, embracing the beauty of life, and protecting the sanctity of our inner garden. Investing in our energetic health is essential for leading with authenticity and compassion, creating relationships that are healthier, more vibrant, and more fulfilling. This approach enhances our connections and enriches our lives, sparking a cycle of positivity that radiates outward.

Saltwater Aura Cleanse Shower Ritual

Purpose: To release stagnant energies, cleanse negativity, and invite renewal while respecting the sacred flow of energy through your body.

1. **Prepare the Space:**
   - Sprinkle sea salt at the bottom of your shower, ensuring it doesn't come into direct contact with your crown. The salt will work from the shoulders down to cleanse and purify.
   - Stand outside the shower and take three deep breaths to ground yourself.
   - Set your intention by saying aloud or silently:
   - "May this water cleanse any stagnant energies that do not serve my highest purpose and renew me with vitality and light."

2. **Step Into the Water:**
   - Turn on the cold water and step in, allowing it to cascade over your body like a gentle waterfall.
   - Close your eyes and imagine a stream of luminous, purifying water flowing from above your crown to your toes, encompassing your entire aura.

3. **Stretch and Release:**
   - Raise your arms high above your head, inviting fresh, vibrant energy through your fingertips.
   - Simultaneously, visualize any negativity, burdens, or stagnant energy exiting through your toes, grounding into the earth below.

4. **Avoid Direct Salt on the Crown:**
   - Gently scoop water from the shower over your shoulders, ensuring the salt-infused water flows only from the shoulders down.
   - As the water moves, envision it carrying away all negativity, heaviness, and old energy.

5. **Visualize the Cleansing:**
   - Picture the water washing away anything that no longer serves you—illness, fears, doubts, or burdens.
   - See these energies dissolving into the water and disappearing down the drain.
   - Recite a cleansing mantra:
     "I release what no longer serves me. I am cleansed, renewed, and radiant."

6. **Feel the Flow of Renewal:**
   - Imagine fresh energy entering your body through your fingertips and spreading throughout your being, filling you with peace, clarity, and light.
   - Breathe deeply, letting gratitude flow with each inhale.

7. **Seal the Cleanse:**
   - Turn off the water and stand for a moment, feeling lighter and more aligned.
   - Whisper a final affirmation:
     "I am whole, vibrant, and ready to step into my highest self."

7. **Complete the Ritual:**
   - Dry yourself gently, recognizing the towel as a symbol of your new, vibrant energy.
   - Thank the water and the salt for their healing properties, and carry this sense of renewal into your day.

This gentle yet intentional approach ensures respect for the energy of the crown while effectively cleansing the aura. Let me know if you'd like additional affirmations or steps!

Navigating Through Shame

Shame is like a silent shadow, lingering in the background of our lives, quietly weighing us down until we take the time to confront it. Unlike guilt, which arises from specific actions, shame feels deeply personal—it whispers that there's something inherently wrong with us. It's not just a feeling we carry on our own; shame often echoes through generations, reflecting unspoken wounds from our ancestors or societal expectations that have been imposed on us. It's an energy that shapes how we see ourselves and how we show up in the world. I like to think of shame as wearing someone else's clothes—they might fit, but they're uncomfortable and not made for you. Sometimes, shame shows up in the expectations placed on us by family, society, or even our younger selves. Take one of my clients as an example. She told me she was studying to become a nurse, but when our conversation shifted to theater, her whole energy transformed. She lit up talking about her love for acting and how she'd always dreamed of being on stage. When I asked why she didn't lead with that, she admitted she'd buried that dream long ago because it wasn't practical, and her parents had never supported it. Shame had convinced her to hide the part of herself that felt most alive.

The first step to healing shame is acknowledging it. This means looking at where it comes from—whether it's rooted in family, society, or past experiences. Ask yourself, *"Is this shame truly mine, or is it something I've inherited or absorbed?"* Once we identify the source, we can begin to release it, forgiving ourselves and others, and breaking free from the chains that hold us back. Shame often travels through our lineage. Our ancestors, though human and flawed, were navigating their own challenges with the knowledge they had at the time. Recognizing this can help us approach their legacies with compassion. By doing so, we don't just heal ourselves; we heal the thread that connects us to those who came before us and those who will come after. This act of forgiveness—of them and of ourselves—is a radical step toward freedom.

Breaking free from shame requires us to redefine who we are on our terms. It's about peeling away the layers of expectations and asking, *"What are my core values?"* It's an invitation to shed the roles and identities we've adopted to please others and step into the truest version of ourselves. When we align our actions and choices with our values, we reclaim our power and begin living a life that feels authentically ours. Living authentically is the ultimate act of courage, and it's the antidote to shame. It means standing firm in who you are, even when the world expects you to be someone else. It's not easy, but it's worth it because it allows us to step out of the shadows and into the light of our own truth.

Shame is a deep and often hidden emotion that whispers we're not enough, that at our core, we're flawed. Unlike the fleeting feelings of guilt or embarrassment, shame digs deep into our spirit, suggesting not just that we've done wrong, but that we are wrong. It's tied to our innermost insecurities, affecting us on physical, emotional, and mental levels. Whether it's triggered by our actions, the words of others, or societal pressures, shame focuses intensely on who we are, not just what we do. It's a shadow that can cloud our vision, making it hard to see our own light or the path ahead. Guilt arises when we stray from our path, acting in ways that conflict with our values and the harmony of our community. It's the heart's way of letting us know we've made a misstep, an acknowledgment that we've acted out of tune with the rhythm of life. Unlike shame, guilt is about our actions and their impact on our relationships. It carries the weight of remorse and the desire for atonement, urging us to mend the tear in the fabric of our connections. Guilt is a teacher, guiding us back to our true path and reinforcing our commitment to live in alignment with our values. Embarrassment is the little nudge we feel when we step out of sync with the social dances around us. It's that warmth in our cheeks when we're momentarily exposed or vulnerable in front of others. Embarrassment speaks to those moments when we drift from our values or the expectations of those around us, yet it's as fleeting as a passing breeze. While uncomfortable, embarrassment is a sign of our humanity and our desire to belong, to stay connected with those we care about. It reminds us of our imperfections and teaches us the grace of humility and the gift of laughter.

Understanding the differences between shame, guilt, and embarrassment helps us walk through life with greater awareness. Shame calls for a journey inward, a path of healing and acceptance to dissolve the clouds of unworthiness. Guilt is a signal to realign our actions with our values, to make amends and restore balance. Embarrassment, with its fleeting touch, reminds us of the joy and humility in being part of the human family. By listening to and learning from each of these emotions, we can step more fully into our power, moving beyond the shadows of shame, learning from the lessons of guilt, and navigating the passing storms of embarrassment with ease. This deeper understanding allows us to live with integrity, ensuring that our actions are in harmony with both the earth and our hearts.

Exercise: Reflecting on Relationships and Energy

Prepare the Space:
- Begin by listing six names of people you've interacted with recently. These can be friends, family members, or colleagues.

Prepare the Space:
- Next to each name, write down how you felt around them the last time you hung out. Were you uplifted, drained, indifferent? This step is crucial for tapping into your emotional response and energy exchange during those interactions.

Conversation Content:
- For each person, jot down what your conversations were primarily about. This could range from casual chit-chat to deep, meaningful discussions. The nature of your conversations often reflects the depth and quality of the relationship.

Unconditional vs. Conditional Love:
- Reflect on each relationship and next to it, write if you consider your love for this person to be unconditional or conditional. This distinction can help you understand the foundation and expectations within each relationship.

Making Space for Love:
- Reflect on how this visual representation can guide you in making space for more love in your life. Identifying and possibly moving on from relationships that are predominantly draining or conditional can open up space for more nurturing, positive connections. Consider how each relationship serves you and whether it aligns with the kind of energy you wish to cultivate in your life.

Insight and Transformation:
This exercise isn't just about identifying the "good" and "bad" relationships but understanding the dynamic interplay of energy within your personal network. It's a step towards recognizing our own role in these energy exchanges, encouraging us to be more mindful of the influence we wield and the spaces we choose to nurture.

For those sensitive to the energies around us, this exercise can be particularly enlightening. It underscores the importance of being selective with our emotional and energetic investments, ensuring we're not only guarding our well-being but also contributing positively to the collective aura of our circles.

By engaging in this reflective practice, we take a meaningful step towards fostering deeper, more vibrant relationships. It's about cultivating an awareness of the energy we both give and receive, guiding us towards interactions that are enriching, supportive, and in harmony with our desires for mutual growth and understanding. This conscious cultivation of our social and emotional environments can lead to a more balanced, fulfilled life.

Activation for Code Five: Harmony and Heart-Centered Living

In this code, we delved into the significance of fostering authentic connections through meaningful communication. By healing and balancing tour authentic expression we enhance our ability to connect genuinely and deeply with others and through what we share and do. We explored practices such as mindful speaking, active listening, and setting clear boundaries to cultivate trust and respect in relationships. Additionally, we discussed the importance of self-discovery and reinvention in releasing shame and aligning with our core values, ultimately allowing us to live authentically and enrich bonds with others and the world we move through.

Affirmations For Integrating Code Five:

- *"My authentic self-expression is my greatest gift to the world. I communicate with honesty, kindness, and compassion, fostering meaningful connections in every interaction."*

- *"I trust in the power of my voice to convey my truth and connect with others on a profound level. My words are a reflection of my inner wisdom and integrity."*

- *"I set clear boundaries that honor my needs and values, allowing me to engage in relationships with authenticity and respect. Through mindful communication, I cultivate trust and mutual understanding."*

- *"I embrace the journey of self-discovery and reinvention, releasing shame and embracing my true essence. By aligning with my core values, I live with integrity and authenticity, enriching my connections with others."*

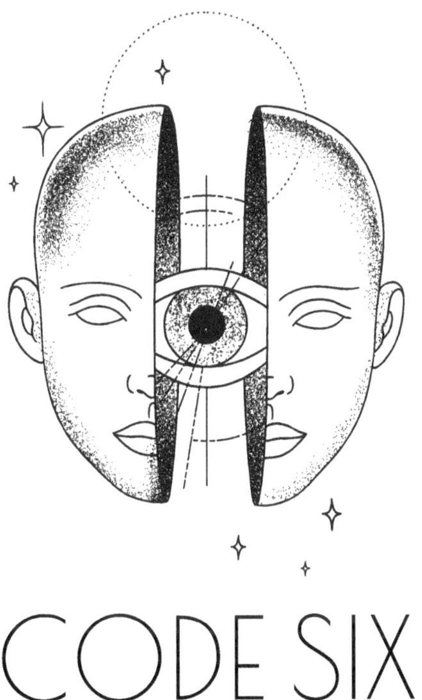

CODE SIX

Connecting to Source & Awakening your Gifts

Code six marks a deep dive into intuition, representing our innate ability to grasp truths beyond conscious reasoning. By reaching this stage, you're ready to fully embrace and trust your inner guidance. You've done that work on yourself and handled business in your hands. This code is about tuning into the subtle nudges and whispers of your soul, recognizing intuition as a powerful, direct line to higher wisdom and it is not for the weak.

To engage with this code, practices such as meditation, mindfulness, and journaling become key. They quiet the mind and amplify your inner voice, helping you to connect more deeply with your intuitive self.

Code six is an encouragement to trust in the unseen, knowing it leads to personal fulfilment and a greater connection with the cosmic flow.

Truth Seekers

Throughout history, many powerful empires and leaders have relied on legendary figures that you might not have known were , astrologers, spiritual advisors, and seers to help make significant political decisions. These individuals, often attributed with mystical insight or profound wisdom, played crucial roles in shaping the course of history. These examples show how figures reputed for their spiritual, mystical, or intellectual insight have been integral to the decision-making processes in various cultures and eras. Their influence often stemmed from their ability to provide counsel that resonated with the spiritual and cultural beliefs of their time, illustrating the intersection of mysticism, politics, and power throughout history.This group of astrologers, spiritual advisors, and seers—who were pretty much the ancient world's version of wisdom gurus. They were the behind-the-scenes influencers, whose wisdom and insight have been key to shaping the course of history, proving that the spiritual and the temporal realms have been interconnected long before hashtags and viral tweets made their mark.

In the narratives of power that dominate our world, there's a persistent growing to a roar suggesting that forces at play would rather keep us unaware of our true potential to keep us small. The exclusion of these varied spiritual practices from mainstream acceptance isn't just about religious or cultural preferences—it's a commentary on how power dynamics shape our understanding of spirituality and our place within the universe.

It's clear that the art of seeking guidance from those with mystical insight isn't just a chapter from history.

There's a movement towards reclaiming our power, recognizing the vast potential within each of us, and embracing the diverse ways humans have always sought to connect with something greater than themselves. This awakening is a journey back to our roots, an exploration of the depth of our souls, and a challenge to the narratives that seek to confine our understanding of the world and our abilities.

The spectrum of individuals endowed with the gift of insight is vast and varied, encompassing seers, witches, wizards, prophets, those who embark on vision quests, fortune tellers, clairvoyants, mediums, practitioners of shamanism, medicine people, and those who connect with totems. These individuals navigate realms beyond the ordinary, tapping into intuition, empathy, and a profound connection with the universe. Yet, among these, mainstream narratives often legitimize only a select few, such as prophets within the frameworks of Christianity, Islam, and Judaism, who are recognized for receiving divine messages about the future or moral directives.

It's clear that the art of seeking guidance from those with mystical insight isn't just a chapter from history.

Imagine standing atop the tallest building in your city, the horizon stretched out before you, and witnessing the harrowing approach of war toward your city. This moment, poised between action and observation, serves as a powerful metaphor for the untapped potential within us all. Would you stand immobilised, watching as the world you know begins to unravel? Or would you race down, rallying others to prepare and protect the community ?This choice encapsulates the profound impact and responsibility that come with recognizing and harnessing our stellar inner powers we all carry.Creator, in painting us in His own image, surely infused us with a spark of His infinite wisdom and magic. It's a divine inheritance, a reminder that we are more than mere physical beings navigating a material world; we are vessels of a higher power, capable of extraordinary feats of insight, healing, and transformation.

"The eye sees only what the mind is prepared to comprehend"

The Highest Form of Vibration

Have you ever been in a bustling room full of noise and distraction, yet effortlessly sent a silent message across the space, received with a knowing smile? Or consider those moments of deep connection established through nothing more than a shared gaze, where words become redundant. This isn't the realm of fantasy but a profound human capability rooted in the highest vibration of our very being and our connection to the divine. Telepathy is the direct transmission of thoughts, feelings, or knowledge from one person to another without using

the traditional senses or physical interaction. It's about tuning
into a specific frequency where the sender and receiver are
synchronized on the same wavelength, allowing for the exchange
of information through mental or emotional vibrations, bypassing
conventional speech or body language. When truly tapped in, you
realize that you can speak a thousand words, but most can only
hear you vibrationally.

Light language is a form of non-verbal communication
that transcends the conventional boundaries of spoken words,
connecting directly with the soul or spirit. A universal language
of energy, it is understood by all on a soul level, regardless of
one's native language or cultural background. This language can
manifest through various expressions such as sound, gestures,
symbols, or written forms, each carrying its unique vibrational
energy and intention. Think of Sanskrit—the Language of the
Gods. It's more than just a collection of words; it's a gateway to
higher realms of consciousness. By immersing ourselves in the
timeless wisdom of Sanskrit, we align with the divine order of
the universe, awakening dormant potentials and expanding our
awareness beyond the limitations of the mundane.

Many of us hesitate to hear our own voices or move
our bodies freely due to self-imposed restrictions or societal
expectations. Growing up with a specific accent or in a particular
cultural setting might influence how we allow ourselves to speak
or act around others, often masking our true selves. To truly
activate this level of communication, you need to embrace your
authentic voice and natural body movements. This could mean
allowing yourself to experience different accents or expressions
of speech or discovering how your body naturally wants to move,
whether through dance or other forms of physical expression. It's
about breaking down the barriers of self-censorship and inviting
a deeper connection with your inner self. Opening ourselves
to receive from our creator isn't just about individual healing;
it's about fostering a deeper connection with the collective
consciousness of all beings.

Connecting with nature is another crucial aspect of activating
light language. This connection can be as simple as observing
a rock in the park, feeling the ocean's water, or letting sand run
through your fingers. These interactions invite a communion with
the natural world, offering insights and energies that can stimulate
the awakening of your light language. Meditation, coupled with

these nature engagements, gradually tunes you into the subtle frequencies of light language, allowing you to start expressing it in ways that resonate with you, such as mimicking the sound of the ocean or the rustling of leaves. Sound and energy healing are profound forms of vibrational communication. Sacred sounds, mantras, symbols, and rituals connect us with the divine, enhance spiritual awareness, and promote healing. Sound healing, in particular, operates on the fundamental principle that everything in the universe, including ourselves, is composed of energy vibrating at different frequencies. By engaging in practices such as sound healing or communicating in light language, we're not just working with vibrations or symbols; we're attuning ourselves to the cosmic symphony of creation.

Research has shown that different frequencies can affect cellular functions such as metabolism, proliferation, and even gene expression. This means that the vibrations we expose ourselves to can directly impact the health and vitality of our cells. Vibrational and energetic healing can reduce stress, alleviate pain, and improve overall well-being by modulating brainwave activity and promoting relaxation. Emerging biofield science explores the subtle energy fields that surround and permeate living organisms. This research suggests that our bodies are not just biochemical machines but intricate systems of energy and information exchange. By working with these biofields through practices such as energy healing, we can facilitate profound shifts in our physical, emotional, and spiritual health.

Our connection to the divine is key in all of this. It's about opening ourselves up to receive the guidance and wisdom of our creator. At the core of this process lies the recognition of our crown, the energy center located at the top of the head, often depicted as a lotus flower blossoming towards the heavens. This is the gateway to the divine, our direct line of communication with the creator, the universe, or however one might perceive the ultimate source of all existence. In this sacred dance of giving and receiving, our role is not just that of a passive recipient but an active co-creator, consciously aligning ourselves with the divine will and allowing it to flow through us.

To be a teacher and inspire others, we must first be a student. This means allowing ourselves to be vulnerable enough to acknowledge that we are always learning and growing, no matter how far we may have come on our journey. Each new experience, each new lesson, is an opportunity for expansion and evolution. As we make space for new feelings and experiences, we create fertile ground for healing to take root and flourish. It's about embracing the full spectrum of human emotion, allowing ourselves to feel deeply and fully, without judgment or resistance. In this space of vulnerability and authenticity, we become conduits for divine wisdom and healing energy to flow through us, illuminating our path and guiding us toward wholeness.

Investing in an energetic mentor—a trusted guide who can hold you accountable, call you out on your made-up stories and poor attitude, and inspire you to take actionable steps—is invaluable. Recognizing our interconnectedness with all beings and taking responsibility for the impact of our thoughts, words, and actions on the world around us is essential. A life coach, someone who embodies the qualities and values that you admire and who has walked the path before you, can offer guidance and support based on their own experiences. Even a skilled therapist can help you uncover patterns and beliefs that may be holding you back, allowing you to break free from old habits and create a life that aligns with your deepest values and aspirations.

Accountability is not just about looking outward; it's also about looking inward—having the courage to confront our own shadows and acknowledge the areas where we may fall short of our ideals. Allowing yourself to be wrong and staying receptive to the messages of our creator and the guidance of our mentors enables you to embrace the role of both student and teacher, continually seeking knowledge and wisdom in all its forms. As we make space for new feelings and experiences, we trust in the transformative power of vibrational healing to lead us toward our highest potential.

Delulu

Most of us intuitively understand that the true essence of sight transcends the physical realm, reaching far beyond what our eyes can perceive. Our consciousness, closely linked to the frontal lobe of the brain, functions as a spiritual lens through which we interpret the world around us. This sacred viewpoint is not solely reliant on visual cues but also on the subtle vibrations and frequencies that permeate all of creation. Such wisdom suggests that our connection with the natural world, and particularly with animals, is a form of telepathic communion. Consider the dolphins, who navigate realms that lie beyond our ordinary senses. These beings, often seen as symbols of higher wisdom, guide us toward the understanding that true sight is an inner journey, one that reveals the deeper layers of reality hidden from ordinary view.

The brain's frontal lobe, known for its role in decision-making, problem-solving, and behavioral control, is more than just a cognitive processor—it is a gateway to deeper perception and spiritual connection. This is what I refer to as Code Six, an inner portal that grants access to profound knowledge and intuition. Awakening this spiritual vision requires a willingness to see beyond the material world, to acknowledge that the universe is far more expansive than what meets the eye. Code Six embodies the profound realization that our dreams, aspirations, and visions are not mere figments of our imagination; they are realities waiting to be embraced and manifested. The unique insights we receive— gifts bestowed upon us by the Creator—have the power to unveil solutions to our most perplexing challenges. But, and this is crucial, these insights can only serve us if we remain grounded and centered.

This is where the importance of the root chakra, or what I call Code One, becomes evident. The root chakra is our connection to the Earth, our anchor in the physical world. It represents our foundation, the bedrock upon which all spiritual and physical growth depends. Without a strong and balanced root chakra, the insights and visions we receive can lead us into realms of delusion, where wishful thinking takes the place of true vision. You can only ascend as highly as you are rooted—imagine, if you will, the crown chakra and the root chakra as two magnetized stars. The root chakra, positioned beneath our feet, keeps us centered and grounded, while the crown chakra, hovering above our head, connects us to the infinite sky world. Between these two points lies the third eye, the seat of spiritual sight, which acts as the gear that harmonizes and integrates these energies. The third eye is the compass, guiding us along the path of spiritual insight, but it can only function properly if both our root and crown chakras are in balance.

Grounding, therefore, is not just a spiritual practice; it is a necessity. Without it, we risk losing ourselves in the illusions of the mind, disconnected from the reality that sustains us. The popular phrase "Don't be Delulu" serves as a modern reminder of this ancient wisdom. Delusions and falsehoods often arise from desires that are self-centered, lacking the universal connection and benefit that genuine visions provide. To distinguish between true spiritual insight and mere fantasy, it is essential to consider the purpose and impact of our visions. Are they self-serving, driven by ego and personal gain? Or do they carry the potential to benefit all of creation, reflecting a commitment to the well-being of the community, the planet, and all living beings?

This discernment is not always easy, but a useful measure is to evaluate the broader impact of the vision. If a vision serves only the self, it may be driven by ego, rooted in the shallow soil of personal desire. However, if a vision has the potential to uplift, heal, and benefit humanity as a whole, it is more likely to be a genuine insight from a place of higher consciousness, guided by divine wisdom. Understanding this distinction encourages us to see the world not just as it is, but as it could be. It reminds us that our perceptions are powerful tools, shaping the reality we experience and the future we create.

Ultimately, the balance between our earthly roots and our celestial aspirations is what allows us to navigate the spiritual path with clarity and purpose. The root chakra keeps us grounded in reality, ensuring that our visions are practical and attainable, while the crown chakra opens us to the infinite possibilities of the universe. The third eye, with its ability to perceive beyond the physical, acts as the guiding force, helping us to discern truth from illusion. By maintaining this balance, we can ascend to great spiritual heights while remaining firmly rooted in the wisdom of the Earth. In this way, we honor both our human and divine nature, creating a harmonious and fulfilling life that serves not only ourselves but all of creation.

How to See a Miracle

Miracles are like whispers from the Creator—gentle yet profound moments that shatter the boundaries of what we think is possible. Do you believe in miracles? And if so, have you ever paused to notice one?

By definition, a miracle is something extraordinary, improbable, and beyond the natural order of things. It's not just a rare occurrence; it's an event so unexpected and transformative that it takes our breath away. But here's the paradox: the very essence of a miracle is that it can't be anticipated. If you're sitting there waiting for a miracle to arrive, clutching onto expectation, you might miss it entirely—because miracles aren't about predictability. They're about divine timing and the infinite possibilities of the unseen.

As humans, we are wired for logic and reason. We crave explanations, patterns, and a sense of control over our lives. That's why the idea of miracles can feel elusive—something that happens to other people or exists only in ancient stories. But miracles are not limited to sacred texts or faraway tales. They are woven into the fabric of everyday life, present in every breath we take and every sunrise we witness. The fact that we are alive, here, in this moment, is nothing short of miraculous.

To truly witness miracles, we have to let go of fear—the fear of the unknown, the fear of being wrong, the fear of believing in something greater than ourselves. We must step out of the comfort zone of logic and into the vast mystery of the Creator's world. This means opening our hearts, quieting our doubts, and daring to see beyond what our eyes reveal. It's about grounding ourselves in faith while staying open to the magic that surrounds us.

Indigenous wisdom teaches us that miracles are not rare—they're part of life's natural rhythm. The wind, for example, is seen as a sacred messenger, carrying prayers to the Great Spirit. The rising sun, the whisper of leaves, the earth beneath our feet—these aren't just mundane occurrences but reminders of the divine at work. Miracles, like the wind, are subtle yet powerful, always moving, guiding, and responding to our needs in ways we may not always understand.

One of the greatest barriers to experiencing miracles is our obsession with control. We try to predict, plan, and dictate every outcome, leaving little room for the unexpected. But life isn't meant to be entirely within our grasp. If we could even begin to grasp a fraction of the unseen forces at play, we'd see just how miraculous existence truly is.

A Miracle to Remember

I've witnessed miracles with my own eyes, and one that remains etched in my memory happened when I was just nine years old. It was during my father's fourth marriage that I learned

I'd be getting a younger brother. Although I had several stepsisters and an older half-sister, I'd pretty much grown up as an only child. The thought of finally having a sibling to share life with was so exciting.

My brother was born a few weeks after 9/11, a time when the world felt chaotic and heavy. He arrived as a healthy baby boy, but something wasn't right. The doctors told us his head had been slightly misplaced during birth, and after a few months of observation, we were informed that he would need surgery. The procedure was scheduled for his first birthday.

Growing up, I spent summers in Costa Rica, where my stepdad was from. It was a place that always felt sacred to me, and during one of those trips, I became fascinated with the story of *La Negrita*, Our Lady of the Angels. *La Negrita* is a small, brown statue of the Virgin Mary holding baby Jesus, believed to have miraculous powers. Legend has it that a young girl, Juana, discovered the statue on a rock in the forest. She brought it home, but it kept mysteriously disappearing and returning to the rock where it had been found. Even when placed in a church tabernacle, the statue would vanish and reappear at the same spot. This was taken as a sign that the Virgin Mary wanted a shrine built there, and today, *La Negrita* is the centerpiece of a grand basilica in Cartago, Costa Rica, surrounded by stories of miraculous healings.

At the basilica, they sell small gold representations of human body parts. It's said that if you purchase one corresponding to an area of illness or injury and pray over it with faith, La Negrita can bring healing. With my baby brother's surgery approaching, I felt a pull to act. I bought a small gold medallion shaped like a head and prayed with all the sincerity and hope my nine-year-old heart could muster.

The next day, I flew back home to Miami and handed the medallion to my dad. That night, we placed it by my brother's crib and prayed together. I remember looking at my baby brother, his tiny head shaved in preparation for the surgery scheduled the next day, and feeling both helpless and hopeful.

And then it happened. Within minutes—yes, minutes—we received a phone call from the hospital. It was late, around 10 PM, but the doctor had urgent news: my brother's surgery was no longer needed. I can still hear the relief and joy in my dad's voice as he relayed the message. It felt like the world had shifted in that moment.

Today, my brother is healthy, thriving, and—like any good little brother—driving us crazy in the best ways.

Miracles have a way of breaking through our fear and doubt, reminding us that the supernatural isn't separate from our lives but deeply interwoven into them. They show us that what seems impossible is, in fact, possible when faith meets divine timing.

La Negrita's story and my brother's healing taught me that miracles don't have to be grand or dramatic to be real. They happen when we least expect them, often in the quiet moments when we surrender control and trust in something greater than ourselves. They remind us of the boundless potential of the human spirit and the profound mysteries of the Creator's hand in our lives.

The thing about miracles is that they rarely come in the form we expect. They're magnetic, pulling unexpected blessings into our lives when we least anticipate them. But here's the key: you have to believe, or at the very least, remain open. Even if you doubt their existence, miracles don't stop happening. They unfold quietly, beautifully, and often without fanfare, as if to remind us that life itself is an ongoing act of divine creation.

Miracles are real. They are the Creator's way of showing us that no matter how dark or impossible things may seem, there is always light, always grace, always the potential for something extraordinary. To see a miracle, you don't need perfect faith or understanding. You just need open eyes, an open heart, and the courage to believe in the infinite possibilities of the world around you.

"Prayer is the highest form of gratitude"

Predictions That Do Not Serve You

Have you ever visited a fortune-teller or encountered someone who predicts your future? Sometimes, these predictions don't necessarily come from a fortune-teller, a witch, or a medium. It could be a random person or a relative sharing their thoughts or feelings about what they think or feel your outcome might be. Sometimes, it's not even someone we know but our very own inner thoughts giving us false predictions, anxiety?

A prediction is essentially a guess, using available information or clues to anticipate what will happen next. For many, especially women, this intuition is a powerful third eye, a silent guide that whispers truths. But the real truth is sometimes we are wrong; the mind can play tricks on us due to our inability to see and receive the proper information.

This is where the dance between the seen and the unseen, the known and the unknown, plays out, teaching us the importance of discernment and clarity. How do we differentiate between a shadow passing and a true sign from the Great Spirit?

Having a clear mind helps us see the truth and choose paths that really matter to us. This clarity is super important because it helps us distinguish what's real from what's not, especially when it comes to predictions about our future. Sometimes, people might tell us things about our future that don't really help or empower us. If we're not careful, these false predictions can lead us to jump to conclusions and start living in a kind of false reality where we're worried or stressed about things that haven't happened and might never happen.

Imagine someone tells you something negative about your future. If your mind isn't clear, you might start believing it's true without any real proof. You begin to worry, making decisions based on this fear rather than what you actually want or what's really happening. This is like living in a bubble of false reality, guided by fear rather than your own hopes and dreams.

To avoid this, it's crucial to keep our minds clear and focused on what we truly know and believe. This means taking a step back from predictions that don't serve us, questioning them, and trusting our own intuition and the real, tangible experiences we have. By doing this, we can avoid falling into the trap of living our lives based on fears or false ideas and instead create a life that's true to who we are and what we genuinely want.

Shawn Stevenson once said, "Never believe a prediction that does not empower you." This wisdom rings true, especially when considering his own story of defying the odds set against him at birth. His journey reminds us that our stories are not written in the stars but crafted by the moments we choose to rise, the paths we dare to walk.

Predictions are reflections, possibilities that challenge us to leap into the unknown with courage, to embrace the uncertainty with an open heart. This realization invites us to live not in fear but in wonder, to embrace each day with the curiosity of a child wandering through life.

We constantly make predictions in our minds, leading us to jump to conclusions. We compile all the clues we've gathered when unsure about the future, allowing ourselves to live in fear. This fear is born from panic-inducing predictions like, "What's going to happen next?" We assemble these unreal clues and rely on disempowering predictions.

Consider this: "The mind is a tool for exploration, not for concluding." As we leap to conclusions, we cease exploring, convinced that "this is it," often stubbornly. This mindset, whether about a political ideology or any other belief, is limiting. It prevents us from seeing other opportunities. Our purpose on Earth is to live in peace, keeping our minds open and constantly exploring, without adhering strictly to any party, ideology, or concocting spiritual laws.

Creating spiritual laws isn't our task. Our role is to wander this Earth, contributing positively, without closing our minds to new ideas or conclusions. Equally, we must not believe everything we hear without question. That's something worth pondering.

Mental Clarity and Authentic Living

Mental clarity is like the clear sky after a storm, offering us the vision to see the stars that guide our journey. This clarity is not just about seeing the path before us but understanding the heart's true calling, distinguishing between the echoes of fear and the voice of our inner truth. Mental clarity acts as the foundation upon which we build our dreams. In a world saturated with noise, distractions, and endless possibilities, finding this clarity is key to discovering a sacred space within, a sanctuary where the whispers of the Great Spirit can be heard with unmistakable clarity.

This clarity is essential, for it allows us to see the truth of who we are and what we are meant to become. To cultivate mental clarity, we must journey inward, embracing solitude and reflection. It's about listening to the silence between the beats of our heart, where the voice of our higher consciousness speaks. As we walk this path, we learn that mental clarity is not just a gift but a responsibility.

Reflective Exercise: Identifying Non-Serving Influences

This concise exercise aims to help you pinpoint and understand the daily inputs—both external and internal—that may not contribute positively to your well-being. Recognizing these can empower you to foster more uplifting thoughts and interactions.

Observation Phase

- **Daily Scan:** Think about a typical day, from morning until night. Consider the types of messages you encounter from people, media, and your own thoughts.

- **Make Notes:** Using your cell phone or another handy device, make brief notes about these messages. Simply tag them as "empowering" or "disempowering." This is about observation, not judgement.

Identifying Non-Serving Voices

- **Highlight Non-Serving:** Review your notes to identify which messages felt disempowering.

- **Reflect Concisely:** For each disempowering message, quickly reflect:
  - Is this within my control?
  - Does it align with my core values?
  - If it's my own thought, what might be the reason behind it?

Shifting Perspective

- **Envision Empowerment:** For each non-serving message, think of an empowering counter-message. If external, how can you limit its impact? If internal, what positive affirmation can replace it?

- **Action Step:** Choose one practical action you will take this week to lessen the impact of a non-serving message and enhance positive influence.

Keeping Track

- **Reminder Setup:** In your phone, set a daily reminder to revisit your empowering counter-messages and action step. This will help integrate your insights into your daily life.

With this exercise, you invite more awareness into the messages that shape your days. By choosing to engage more with empowering thoughts and less with the disempowering ones, you're setting the stage for a more positive and authentic life path.

"THE BLISS OF BEING "

Activation for Code Six: Intuition & Gifts Awakening

This chapter underscores the profound significance of aligning with the divine source and unlocking one's innate intuitive abilities. Throughout the chapter, various insights have been shared, highlighting the timeless dance between the seen and unseen realms, the power of miracles, and the importance of discernment in navigating predictions and spiritual downloads. By embracing practices like meditation, mindfulness, and connecting with nature, individuals can cultivate mental clarity and open themselves to receive guidance from the universe. This journey of awakening not only deepens personal fulfillment but also fosters a greater connection with the cosmic flow, reminding us of our divine gifts and the extraordinary potential within each of us reconnecting us with our essence as spiritual beings and awakening that of source within us all.

Affirmations for Integrating Code Six:

- "I trust in the whispers of my soul and embrace my inner guidance."

- "I open myself to receive spiritual downloads and insights from the universe."

- "I release fear and doubt, allowing miracles to unfold in my life effortlessly."

- "I cultivate mental clarity and discernment, listening to the voice of my higher consciousness."

- "I honor the universal language of light and permit myself to activate its power within me."

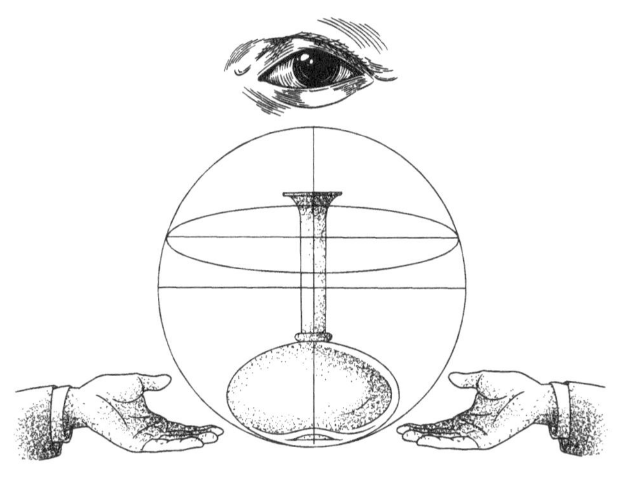

CODE SEVEN

-The Whispering Guidance-

In the stillness, we receive—a crown of silent guidance, woven from the unseen realms. Our crown is more than the center of thought; it is the doorway to divine insight, where the noise of the world fades, and we hear only the whispers of the Creator. Through this sacred portal, we allow wisdom to flow freely, a river of knowing untouched by fear or doubt.

Here, we are reminded to listen deeply, to open ourselves to the messages that rise in quiet moments, guiding our steps with a grace that is ancient and boundless. Each wordless insight, each subtle nudge, is a reminder that we are not alone on this path. We are tuned to a higher frequency, connected to a force greater than ourselves, and in surrender, we let the truth of our purpose unfold

"GRATITUDE IS THE HIGHEST FORM OF PRAYER"

Cultivating Trust

Cultivating trust is like nurturing a sacred bond, where commitment becomes the roots that ground us. When we place trust in a relationship, our job, our passion, or our vision, it becomes the very essence that fuels our journey forward. You might be familiar with the saying, "Trust the Process." This phrase, regardless of one's spiritual beliefs, often brings a sense of relief, a reassurance that, amidst our worries, there's a higher power we can lean on if we find it hard to trust in ourselves.

This understanding, that trust begins within, is pivotal. It has been a guiding light for me, especially in moments of uncertainty. Do I trust myself? Do I trust the unfolding of events in this vast tapestry of existence, especially now, with the world in such flux?

Reflecting on the origins of trust, consider how instinctively we gauge trustworthiness. Meeting someone new, perhaps in an elevator, our comfort levels might shift based on subtle cues, influenced perhaps by their demeanour or even our own intuition. This instinctual process of trust evaluation is fascinating. It begs the question: What is it about someone that tilts our inner scales towards trust or caution? Researchers suggest that certain features might play a role, but beyond physical traits, there's a deeper recognition at play, a soul-level discernment that guides us.

Trust is not merely about the reliability of others but starts with a profound trust in oneself. This lesson, learned through the wisdom of companions along my path, reveals that those who trust easily often do so because they are anchored in their own self-assurance. They trust their judgment, their abilities, and this self-trust naturally extends to those they interact with. It's a reflection of professional confidence; leaders trust their teams because they trust in their own leadership and decision-making.

Yet, at the heart of trust issues lies fear—the fear of undesirable outcomes. This fear is particularly palpable in relationships and professional settings, where past experiences or second-hand stories might cloud our perception of someone. We may hesitate to trust based on a history we haven't directly witnessed, relying instead on narratives that may not empower us. It's essential to discern the root of our hesitations: Are they grounded in our own experiences, or are they shadows cast by the fears and judgments of others?

To trust others, one must embark on the journey of trusting oneself. It's about peeling back the layers of doubt and fear, reaching into the core of our being where a steadfast spirit resides. It's there, in the quietude of our hearts, that we find the strength to trust, to extend our hand in faith and walk together in trust. This path of trust is not walked alone but in the company of all those who have come before us and those who walk beside us, guided by the light of trust that illuminates the way forward.

The inability to trust often stems from a place of fear, a concern about the potential outcomes that might unfold. This apprehension is not uncommon in both personal relationships and professional settings, where we might find ourselves hesitating to place trust in others based on their past actions or the stories we've heard about them. It's akin to navigating through a forest, relying on secondhand maps that might not truly reflect the terrain. Such situations lead us down a path of negative assumptions, where our judgments are clouded by hearsay rather than direct experience.

When we encounter individuals whose reputation precedes them, it's worth pausing to consider the origin of our reservations. Are these feelings rooted in our personal interactions, or are they influenced by the whispers and warnings of others? This reflection is crucial, for relying solely on the perspectives of others can trap us in a cycle of unfounded fears, preventing us from forging potentially meaningful connections.

Indeed, the journey toward trusting others begins with a deep, introspective look at our capacity to trust ourselves. It's about standing at the edge of a great canyon and knowing that the bridge we're about to cross is one we've built from our strength, wisdom, and heart. Trusting oneself is the first step in extending that trust outward, allowing us to walk confidently in the knowledge that we can navigate the complexities of relationships and the professional world with discernment and grace.

To trust is to open ourselves to the possibility of growth and connection, understanding that while not every path will be smooth, our inner compass, honed by self-trust and awareness, will guide us through. It's a journey of leaning into the unknown, supported by the faith we have in ourselves and the potential to see beyond the veils of fear and uncertainty.

Worship

Worship is the sacred act of connecting deeply with the Creator, the Great Spirit who flows through all things. It is an expression of our gratitude for the breath of life, the waters that flow, and the earth that sustains us. Worship is not confined to spoken prayers or the songs we sing; it is lived in our daily actions, in the reverence we show to the earth, and in the respect we offer to all our relations.

In the traditions passed down from generation to generation, worship is understood as walking in harmony with the earth, listening to the whispers of the wind, and observing the teachings of the animals and plants. Each sunrise offers a moment for gratitude, each change of season a reminder of the cycles of life, and each starry night a canvas of the Creator's vastness.

Hindu worship, known as Puja, can be performed through offerings such as flowers, food, and incense. It is both a personal and communal act to express devotion and connect with the divine. Meditation and chanting of mantras are also significant, aiming to elevate the soul towards liberation.

In Judaism, worship is expressed through prayer, the study of the scriptures, and living according to the commandments. In Christianity, worship involves acknowledging God's grace through Jesus Christ. Several passages throughout the Bible offer insight into how God views worship and the importance He places on it: To worship is to surrender to something much greater than your thoughts and habits. Worship is a feeling or expression of reverence and adoration.

In my younger years, Catholic teachings were a constant rhythm in my life, woven into songs and hymns that echoed through our gatherings. Those melodies carried a joy that resonated with my youthful heart, becoming part of the spirit of our assemblies. But as I grew older and found myself stepping into different Christian circles, I felt disconnected. The classical music that once moved me now felt out of place—let's be real, sometimes it came across as too cheesy for me to take seriously. Yet, something unexpected happened. It wasn't the music that brought me back; it was the wisdom woven into the spoken word.

That wisdom rekindled a flame, allowing me to hear the songs in a new way, to feel their power and their connection to something greater.

This experience shifted my perspective and sparked a curiosity in me to explore religions far beyond the one I was raised in. Now, most of the books I read are teachings from Hinduism and Buddhism—paths rich in practices that connect the soul to the divine. Still, I find myself drawn to Christian churches, even though I know I'm not exactly the poster child for their congregation. There's something about hearing the Word and witnessing a community in worship that feels deeply moving, even though I don't always feel fully accepted there.

I've been called a pagan, a term that echoes the language colonizers used to describe Native Americans. But here's the truth: the sun, the moon, the wind, the earth—they are not God, but creations of God. They are portals to source, tangible reminders of the divine. What Native American teachings beautifully convey is the understanding that nature is a sacred bridge, a way to experience and honor the Creator. The sun and moon, as constant presences in our lives, are not objects to be worshipped but reflections of the divine's infinite reach, their light and cycles reminding us of the Creator's rhythm.

This is where Native teachings and many spiritual traditions resonate deeply with us. They teach that the physical world isn't separate from the divine—it's a reflection of it. It's not about idolizing the sun or the moon but recognizing their role as sacred guides, messengers of a Creator who is beyond our full understanding.

So, while I may not fit perfectly into any one religious box, I've come to see that the essence of all these traditions—Christianity, Buddhism, Hinduism, and Indigenous teachings—points to the same truth: that God, or Source, is everywhere and everything. Whether it's in a church pew, a sacred fire, or the rising sun, the Creator speaks to us in ways as vast and varied as the stars in the sky.

"When the Spaniards arrived, they called the Indigenous 'pagans' and accused them of worshipping the devil. The Indigenous, with profound simplicity, replied: 'What is the devil?' A question that revealed not ignorance, but a wisdom untouched by imposed dualities—a worldview that saw divinity in all things, untainted by the fear of shadows."

This understanding of the sacred continues to guide us in honoring our ancestors—a bridge between the past and present. Their struggles, triumphs, and wisdom are etched into our being, but there is a crucial distinction: we honor them, not worship them. Our worship belongs to the Creator, the ultimate source of light and life that flows through all things.

Worship is not just a song or a prayer—it's the way we live. It's in the respect we show to the Earth, the love we give to others, and the humility with which we walk through life. To worship is to devote oneself, not in a way that diminishes, but in a way that elevates. True devotion enriches the self and everything around us, aligning us with the Creator's will and bringing harmony to our communities.

Interestingly, in today's world, 'worship' can feel like a loaded term, as if it somehow takes away from personal autonomy. But real worship—whether through faith, prayer, or simple acts of gratitude—is an act of empowerment. It's not about making demands or striking deals; it's about surrendering with love and trust, committing wholeheartedly to a greater purpose.

This devotion becomes a daily conversation with the Great Spirit—not just in words but in actions, thoughts, and the quiet language of the heart. Worship is reflected in how we treat others, how we honor nature, and how we nurture the sacredness within ourselves. It's not confined to rituals or sacred spaces; it's a way of being, a living prayer that embodies humility, courage, and love.

When we see worship as a commitment to love and respect—for ourselves, for others, and for the Creator—it transforms us. We become vessels of devotion, offering our lives as a testament to the beauty and grace of the world we walk upon. Worship, in its truest form, is an attitude—a life lived in alignment with the sacred."

The Non-Negotiable

In my years of training and developing top performers in the world of sales and marketing, I discovered four key traits that set the best apart. At the top of that list was attitude. I used the sales floor as a laboratory for the most talented and compassionate individuals to tap into their deepest dreams and showed them how to use a job they hated as a stepping stone to make those dreams a reality. Having them truly heal and connect with their deeper self required bravery and truthfulness. The attitude thing was a big one I just could not work with. I always said I could work with no experience, over qualified, traumas, speech impediments, learning disabilities, no leg you name it, but the one thing I would absolutely not tolerate was bad attitude. It blocks the way for our inner wisdom to guide us, not allowing miracles and divine messages to reach us. Harboring a bad attitude can block these positive flows, shutting out any chance for goodness to enter our lives. By embracing our emotions and working through them, we transform our attitude, opening ourselves to a life filled with peace, gratitude, and an eagerness for the wonderful opportunities that lie ahead. This ensures that our path remains open to all the good that seeks us. Someone told me that could never have a bad attitude as long as they remained in constant state of gratefulness because it holds a loving, and humble disposition.

The principle of interconnectedness teaches that our attitudes and actions have ripple effects on the world around us. A bad attitude can contribute to negative outcomes not just for the usl but also for the broader circles of our influence, including our family, community, and the natural world.

This attitude is not merely a surface response but a manifestation of a deeper disconnect from our higher consciousness. It is a signal that we have strayed from the alignment with our true essence, the Great Spirit that guides and nurtures our journey.

Code two teaches us that every emotion is a sacred visitor, deserving of our attention and respect. To suppress or ignore these emotions is to bury them in the soil of our soul, where, like anything that is buried without care, they begin to decay. This decay can spread, contaminating the sacred ground of our being with negativity, which manifests as a pervasive bad attitude. This negativity then acts as a barrier, blocking access into code seven which is the flow of divine messages and miracles that are our birthright, obscuring the signs and guidance that are constantly being offered to us.

Imagine our emotions as seeds; when we allow them to be felt deeply and processed fully, they can be planted in the fertile ground of our understanding. With care and attention, these seeds grow into a garden of wisdom, blooming with insights and blessings. Our crown, the spiritual center connected to the Great Spirit, is then guided not by the rot of unaddressed emotions. This divine connection ensures that our path is illuminated with clarity, allowing miracles to unfold naturally in our lives.

Healing and connecting with our deeper self takes bravery and truthfulness. We must meet our challenges and feelings openly, seeing them as guides. This clears the way for our inner wisdom to lead, making room for the wonders and messages meant for us. Holding onto a bad attitude, however, blocks these blessings, preventing anything good from coming our way. By deeply feeling and healing our emotions, we change our outlook, welcoming life with peace, thankfulness, and a readiness for the amazing things ahead, ensuring our path is open to all that is good.Unlocking code seven requires us to ensure that code two is truly felt, that all our emotions are truly and deeply felt and processed so that our crown is geared by our great spirit.

*"Every emotion that you cannot express, you bury.
Everything you bury rots
Everything that rots smells "*

TD JENKINS

The Infinite Path

To surrender means to cease resistance to an enemy or opponent and submit to their authority." The above definition doesn't seem glamorous at all. When I first read it, I told myself that I'd never want to submit to any kind of authority. However, you have to ask yourself who the authority is that you must submit to.

Stay receptive with me now, It's about opening ourselves up to the whispers of the universe, listening intently to the subtle cues and nudges that guide us on our path. This receptivity requires a sense of surrender, a willingness to let go of preconceived notions and embrace the unknown with open arms.

Consider it your first day of a new job that you are super excited about as its in a space where you will be able to level up, and you answer to a new boss; it incites a sense of accountability, not fear. When you show up to a new job you must accept that you know nothing and will follow under new management styles and work cultures.

Hence, it creates a balance in such an environment, which makes the idea of answering to an authority good. If there's no authority to be accountable to in the workplace, things might go haywire

. Who is the authority that you follow? Some people will say they don't answer to anybody. As for me, my biggest boss is my Creator. Surrendering to the authority that I trust is the biggest form of gratitude, trust, detachment, and forgiveness. I believe that to live this blissful life, I must surrender to my authority. When I submit to God or my higher consciousness, as soon as unpleasant thoughts cross my mind, I stop.

There are times when I catch myself feeling anxious or stressed, I like to hold myself accountable to not let such things happen to me, and if it does, it's only for a few hours. So when it does happen, I just tell myself to surrender because I'm not even in charge in the first place.

To surrender, you must truly learn to trust the process. When you do not trust, that's when you freak out and create anxiety, stress, and all the negative things going on in your head. You need to learn to let go of control. You must not be in control all the time. Funnily, I am guilty of being a control freak too. We feel like we need to deliver on things that just crossed our minds. However, in actuality, if you give yourself an opportunity for things to coexist and happen regardless of what you think you have to do, the universe will deliver it. If you can let go, whatever it is that you've imagined and think you're duty-bound to do, the universe can deliver it better than you ever could.

If you've met older people, they may be able to offer a broader perspective on this matter. My granny always talks about how her life turned out better than she ever intended. She'd talk about how she's had beautiful children, grandchildren, and a more splendid life than she planned for herself. That always reminds me that no matter what we imagine, the universe is capable of giving us tenfold more. To surrender, we need to trust ourselves and God.

To surrender is also to forgive. Forgive people for the hurt they caused you, whether your parents or a classmate from elementary school; forgive all. Forgiveness doesn't mean you have to forget, but it gives you permission to feel whatever you didn't feel at that moment. It is a form of surrendering. You surrender to the fact that something happened, but you are still moving on. Forgive yourself too. Revisit the points where you feel you offended yourself and make amends if you can. Otherwise, just forgive and move on.

To surrender fully, you must also learn to detach yourself. Detach from ego and all negativities around you. Detach from people's thoughts and perspectives as well. Learn to detach from all things, understanding that nothing is truly yours in the first place.

Gratitude is everything. It's about recognizing that every part of your journey—the highs, the lows, the lessons, and the blessings—is a gift. From the air we breathe to the ground beneath our feet, life itself, our tribes, the moments of pure joy, and even the challenges, they're all treasures from the Universe, shaping our paths. Let's not just keep this appreciation to ourselves. Spread that thankfulness to those who journey with us and, of course, to the Great Spirit, the ultimate source of all these wonders. Living with a heart full of gratitude is how we truly honor the gifts we've been given and the connections we share with everything around us.

To surrender is not merely to yield to an authority but to embrace the guidance of the Great Spirit, the ultimate source of wisdom and love. It is a journey of trusting the path laid before us, recognizing our place in the great cycle of life where every beginning has its teachings and every challenge its purpose. Surrendering means acknowledging that we are but students of the Earth, ready to learn from the myriad lessons she offers. It involves letting go of the illusion of control, opening our hearts to the guidance of the Creator, and finding peace in the understanding that we are part of a greater plan. This act of surrender is a profound expression of trust, gratitude, and acceptance, allowing us to navigate life's journey with humility, to forgive freely, and to detach from the burdens that weigh us down. It teaches us to be grateful for the abundant blessings around us, from the air we breathe to the earth beneath our feet, and to live in harmony with all our relations. In surrendering, we align our spirits with the Creator, finding balance and beauty in the delicate dance of existence.

When I started my first company House of Vibration, one of my biggest concerns was ensuring that I was able to create a space where people of all religions and beliefs could come together to heal. Healing starts with the power of our thoughts and communication with our divine. Whether that be God, Ala, Krishna, Messiah, creator, or simply your highest consciousness. I invite you to read this book as a form of prayer, no matter where your soul takes you, this book is meant to connect you.

Prayer is loud.
Prayer is silent.
Prayer is peace.
Prayer is love.
Prayer is kind.
Prayer is accepting and wholly understanding.
Prayer is yours.
Prayer is bright and forever mine.

Inspiration from Prayer

Prayer is a conversation with our Creator, a moment of connection to the Source of life, the only one who can love us wholeheartedly and unconditionally. The best way to understand prayer is to reflect on how we keep in touch with those we love. We all have that one friend we can talk to every single day about everything, from trivial matters to life's dilemmas and dramas. We have others with whom we speak every other week to catch up on each other's lives and discuss our families. We might grab lunch or have a drink with them occasionally. Some friends come around to celebrate the good times, while others are always there when we need them most, offering a simple word or hug that feels like a lifetime of support. Prayer is understood as the sacred breath that connects us to the Great Spirit, the life force that animates all creation. It is more than words spoken or sung; it is the heart's truest language, a vibrational offering that transcends the seen world and touches the unseen. This sacred communication works hand in hand with spiritual sight, an inner vision that allows us to see beyond the physical realm into the vastness of the spiritual world. This spiritual sight is akin to the concept of the third eye, an inner portal of perception and understanding that opens us to the deeper truths of existence.

This is what prayer represents: timelessness, with no past, no future, no present. Our Creator always has the perfect thing to say to us, whether we reach out once a day, every day, or once every few years. If we hold ourselves accountable for keeping in touch with our friends and family at specific times, why not do the same to maintain a conversation with the most important source of light in our lives? Prayer inspires, reassures, and uplifts us.

The third eye, or the inner eye of wisdom and intuition, is awakened through the practice of prayer and meditation. It allows us to perceive the interconnectedness of all things, to understand the sacredness of life, and to recognize the divine in ourselves and in all creation. With our spiritual sight activated, we see the world not just as a collection of physical experiences but as a vibrant tapestry of energy, spirit, and light. We become aware of the subtle energies that flow through the earth, the plants, the animals, and the air we breathe. We understand that every rock, river, and ray of sunlight is imbued with spirit, and we learn to live in harmony with these forces.

Prayer, then, becomes a powerful tool for nurturing our spiritual sight. It helps us to cultivate a deep, intuitive connection with the Great Spirit, enabling us to walk in balance and beauty. Through prayer, we align our heartbeats with the heartbeat of Mother Earth, we harmonize our spirits with the rhythms of the universe, and we open ourselves to the profound wisdom that resides within and all around us.

In this sacred practice, we acknowledge that the veil between the physical and spiritual worlds is thin, that there is no separation between us and the Great Mystery. We realize that through prayer and the awakening of our spiritual sight, we can navigate both realms with clarity and purpose, guided by the ancient wisdom that has sustained our people through countless generations. This is the path of the true seeker, the one who walks with one foot in both worlds, holding the vision of unity, harmony, and the endless cycle of life.

Prayer bridges the physical world and the spiritual realm. For instance, if you wake up panicked from a nightmare, thinking, "Please, God, never let this be true," you're tapping into a channel deeper than our surface-level existence. Prayer is that bridge between the physical and non-physical worlds, a communication line to the world of dreams and beyond.

Wishful thinking belongs only to the physical realm. Consider prayer as a force of light, a magical key that transitions you from the spiritual to the physical. Remember, God cannot answer a prayer that isn't prayed.

Personally, prayer and meditation go hand in hand for me. The only way I can meditate properly is if I pray first. This allows me to shut off everything else and focus. I start my prayer by giving thanks and expressing gratitude, grounding myself not just for the beauty in my life but also for the challenges that have made me stronger.

Relying solely on prayer without incorporating a moment to receive through meditation can turn prayer into a one-sided demand rather than allowing your Creator to provide answers. It's important to recognize the fine line between instructing God and communicating our desires for manifestation.

Meditation is an opportunity to sit back and say, "I'm going to stop acting like I'm in control and open myself to what's meant for me." It's about faith, not about knowing the 'how' of God's workings. Concerning ourselves with how things will happen is not our role; our job is to have faith and live joyfully.

Heaven focuses on truth, not merely happiness. Truth completes us and aligns us with our destiny. In prayer, it's not necessary to always ask for something in return. Prayer is a conversation, an expression of gratitude, a language filled with the magic of worship.

Our Creator is always eager to hear from us, ready to listen the moment we reach out, whether we've been distant or close. He's there for us, even if we've missed significant moments or broken promises, always welcoming us back with open arms.

Activation for Code Seven: Alignment & Divine Connection

This code invites you into a journey of self-reflection and deeper connection with your highest vision. You've explored that aligning your life with your divine essence requires trust, self-acceptance, and surrender to the guidance that flows within. This journey isn't about seeking out new parts of yourself; it's about discovering what has always been there, waiting to be seen and felt in its entirety. The essence of true alignment comes from seeing beyond the everyday and recognizing that your inner vision is already unfolding in perfect timing.

- *I embrace my journey of constant evolution: I recognize that I am not broken but rather continually expanding and growing in alignment with the divine flow of life.*

- *I trust in divine timing: I surrender to the process of life, knowing that everything unfolds in perfect timing, and I am always guided and supported by the universe.*

- *I am a living prayer, a conduit for divine wisdom: I open myself to receive guidance from the Great Spirit, allowing miracles and blessings to flow effortlessly into my life.*

Reflective Questions:

As you close your eyes, ask yourself: *When I envision my dream life, what do I see?* Is there vibrant imagery, or is there darkness and quiet? If there is darkness, do not fear it; lean in gently. Look closer, and allow patterns and stories to emerge. Do you see old dreams, whispers of past experiences, or feelings waiting to be acknowledged? This is your pineal gland, your inner vision, guiding you to what is already in store. Let this awareness show you where clarity exists, and where deeper knowing wants to come forward.

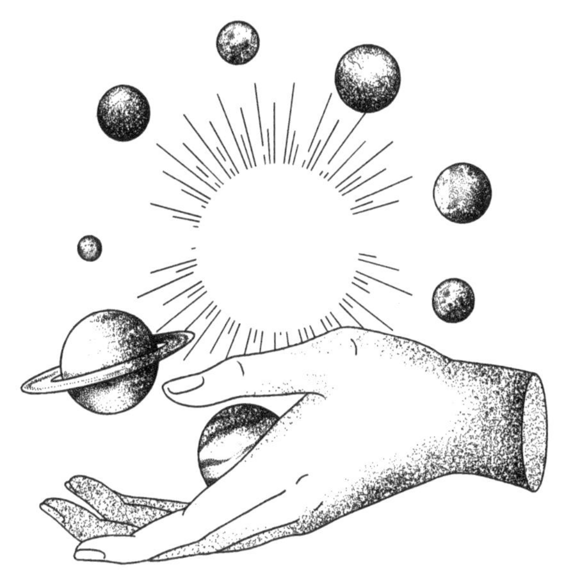

CODE EIGHT

-Your Highest Mission-

What you leave behind

In the quiet depths of eternity, a purpose pulses—an endless river flowing through the vastness of being. Here, right beneath the heavens, we walk in the footsteps of the stars, guardians of a mission woven into the fabric of all creation.

As we stand at the threshold of the infinite, we are reminded: our life is not merely a journey but a calling, a vision held together by threads of love, courage, and boundless possibility. We are the keepers of a truth older than time, travelers charting sacred pathways in every direction—north, south, east, and west.

GIVE GIVE AND YOU SHALL RECEIVE BUT CAN YOU RECEIVE? MANIFESTATION

To have gotten this far is a gift

Transcending visual perception into Code Eight acts as a gateway to infinite wisdom and universal love, unlocking higher states of consciousness and spiritual enlightenment. Imagine it as a mystical key, opening doors to realms where time and space blur, revealing cosmic truths. This connection allows guidance and knowledge to flow like a celestial river, with insights from ancient sages, cosmic entities, and your higher self illuminating your path, trippy right?

Why do we only hear about death as a bad thing? From the moment we enter this world, we're told the only certainty is that to live, you must die. Death is just a portal, a transition to a new cycle. We constantly hear about the world ending, apocalypses, threats of World War III, and people building bunkers out of fear. Many even end their beautiful lives due to panic and lies created by illusion. Why does no one talk about the possibilities of the new world? How precious it will be, how you are a vital source to that utopia.

When I first entered the world of spirituality, I quickly realized that the people in this space were just as lost as those I helped in the corporate world. I mean it—many of these teachers, coaches, gurus, and wellness experts had zero concept of what it took to run a business. Once again, I was faced with being "too businessy" for the energetics space of helping humanity. I started hearing complaints from what I began calling my new co-workers, "the spiritual influencers," that the market was oversaturated. Every time I attended an event or collaborated with another leader, there was a constant feeling of competition. At first, it made me laugh, and I took it lightly. I quickly realized there was more work to be done that I did not anticipate originally.

This entire industry had little experience in working a real job; therefore, they lacked discipline, struggled with authority, and their crown chakra was all kinds of messed up. I realized I had some heavy shoes to fill. Here I was, thinking I would join a mission to help humanity with a team of other healers. Newsflash: I was going to have to start helping my new co-workers with self-worth and abundance. So I made it my responsibility to wear this hat—there were so many of them. I mean, if you went on social media, it felt like everyone was feeling called to lead. Was the market really oversaturated? Then it hit me—this isn't a normal market; this is our planet. Humanity is in dire need of leaders. Now more than ever, this role is essential. It's not that we have too many healers and leaders; we actually need more!

As we shed the illusions of separation and ego, we embrace our identity as integral parts of a vast, interconnected whole. It's like peeling away layers of an onion to reveal a grand design, where every layer has purpose and unity, creating the best onion rings you'll ever eat. Yes, the onion made your eyes water as you sliced it, and yes, your hands and breath smell like onion, but you have to admit it makes a simple meal spectacular. This silly revelation is a glimpse of what it's like to live this life; it empowers us to achieve spiritual maturity and activate our greatest mission on Earth. Picture yourself as a hero in an epic cosmic saga, each step bringing you closer to fulfilling a divine destiny.

Understanding consciousness from a personal to a universal level highlights the profound interconnectedness of all life and our role as co-creators of reality. It's like transitioning from a solitary actor to a playwright, crafting new narratives for the entire ensemble. This shift enriches your personal journey and contributes to humanity's collective ascension.

Now, you might think, "I have no idea what this means." But I promise—you're beginning to understand and take responsibility for your universal role as a starseed, a child of the cosmos. It's like embarking on an enchanted quest where each revelation brings you closer to the heart of the universe. You're a crucial piece in a cosmic puzzle, where every action creates ripples that touch countless lives. So, buckle up and relish the journey! This adventure is filled with awe-inspiring discoveries, boundless wonder, and the profound joy of connecting with the infinite.

Remember, the last test is always the hardest because you realize there is no end to anything. Whether it's a woman's last trimester, the end of a relationship, or quitting a job you hate, the final moments are the most challenging. To have gotten this far is a gift.

Code Eight reminds us that the next step in our spiritual evolution is where the boundaries between self and others begin to dissolve, and we recognize our inherent unity with the cosmos.

As we enter the next code, I want you to envision rays of luminescent white shimmering, an iridescent hue that encapsulates the spectrum of light and the unseen aspects of your physical self. Picture yourself standing at the center of a radiant explosion, where beams of pure light wash over you, enveloping you in a cocoon of sparkling brilliance. Imagine it as if you're being dipped in glitter from head to toe, each particle reflecting a rainbow of colors, creating a dazzling aura that radiates from within. Or, if you prefer a whimsical touch, envision Lisa Frank herself orchestrating a life makeover, transforming your essence into a masterpiece of vibrant, kaleidoscopic splendor. Whatever your heart desires, make it fabulous, allowing your imagination to soar and your spirit to bask in the glow of this magnificent transformation. This vision is not just about outer beauty but a reflection of the inner light and boundless potential within you.

If you haven't noticed by now, news flash: you are powerfully connected to the ability to perform acts of profound healing, both for yourself and others, and to manifest realities that align with the highest good of all. Think about what you're doing—some of you reading this are in finance, nurses, doctors, lawyers, master communicators, social workers, even body hair waxers. I mean, to wax someone is to make them feel comfortable in their most intimate moments—that's a gift. Whatever it is that requires your service, understand that our generation, and those to come, now have the consciousness to heal generational karmas. Just being born, you beat astronomical odds. The odds of being born are about 1 in 400 trillion, considering the unique genetic combinations and precise conditions needed for conception. From a scientific perspective, this highlights the rarity and uniqueness of each life. Spiritually, it suggests a deeper purpose or divine plan, with each individual seen as a crucial part of the universe's interconnected bond. Together, these views inspire awe and gratitude, emphasizing the miracle of existence and our significant role in the cosmic story.

If you can do all of that, why wouldn't you be able to create the exact life you want? Or even something simple, like calming your busy mind from anxiety? Or even healing yourself from traumas, overcoming heartbreak, and breaking toxic patterns when you could simply travel through dimensions? When you get to Code Eight, you understand we are just little stars in an oasis of galactic superstars and planets, each playing a part in the grand cosmic play.

Ignorance is Bliss

I don't know about you, but for a long time, I couldn't stand the fact that it seemed like people got away with being terrible humans. The mean girls in school dated the jocks, drove nice cars, went to the coolest parties, bullied their own friends, and seemed to live perfect lives. Meanwhile, the moment I cracked a joke at their expense or stooped to their level, karma would hit me like a truck. Even in my sales training career, I saw colleagues slacking off, ripping off clients, lying their way through deals, skipping work, and half-assing their jobs. And yet, every time I even thought about following their lead, guilt would consume me, leaving me reflecting on my actions.

Any time I've participated in a not-so-proud moment, I would seek validation from friends or gravitate toward people who shared similar behaviors so we could justify each other's actions. It's a common pattern—you see it at work in cliques that spend lunch breaks trashing their jobs or laughing at happy hour about how they outsmarted the system. It's addictive behavior. I noticed something: these individuals often lack a conscience about the harm they cause. Meanwhile, my hyper-sensitive conscience never allowed me the peace others seemed to enjoy in their blissful ignorance.

We would sit around, rationalizing our behavior, convincing ourselves it was okay because "everyone else does it." But deep down, I knew it was a façade—a way to numb the gnawing guilt that would inevitably surface. Some of you might read this and think, "Thankfully, I don't participate in conflict or bullying, and my business doesn't harm the planet." But have you examined your own thought patterns? When you see someone in need, do you pause to help? Do you take responsibility for your environment? Better yet, how do you perceive yourself? Even negative thoughts create a heaviness in our collective consciousness.

Imagine consciousness as a vast web connecting us all, where each thought and action ripples through the entire structure. Toxic patterns—anger, jealousy, resentment—don't just harm us; they disturb this web, influencing others. Think about how negativity in a workplace spreads, eroding morale and productivity. Social media amplifies this, where one negative post can spark a chain reaction, affecting countless emotional states. It's our spiritual footprint.

Negative thoughts also shape our interactions, influencing our words, body language, and relationships. People intuitively sense our energy, and negativity creates an uneasy aura. If you're reading this and reflecting on moments you're not proud of, that's good—you're learning. Awareness is the first step.

When I was a teenager, I visited a family friend's lake house. Her mother had married an all-American gentleman, and their family was always so kind to me. We spent hours roasting marshmallows, playing cards, and enjoying the lake. For the first time, I didn't feel alienated as a child of immigrants—until one night. While playing cards with my friend's step-grandmother, we were deep in conversation when she stopped us and said, "Before you continue, tuck your hands under your legs." Confused, we complied, thinking it was part of a game. Then she added, "Now try to speak without so much hand movement. That's the thing about Hispanics—they always have to talk with their hands."

My friend and I exchanged shocked glances but remained polite, continuing the game. It was a pivotal moment for me. I knew this woman had no ill intent—she had welcomed me, fed me, and shown me kindness. Yet her ignorance highlighted a belief system passed down through generations. It left a mark. I never confronted her, but it ignited something in me. Today, I proudly use my hands for storytelling and healing, turning that moment of prejudice into a source of power.

These collective negative patterns contribute to societal issues like prejudice and conflict. Groups harboring fear and anger manifest as social unrest and discrimination, burdening the collective consciousness. By cultivating positive thoughts, we can break this cycle. Personal growth doesn't just serve us; it fosters a ripple effect that uplifts those around us, creating a more compassionate world.

So why does it seem like some people get away with everything while others face consequences? After years of reflection, I realized the difference: I always knew better. The Great Spirit holds us accountable for what we know. Every step forward, every good intention, is celebrated. But when we repeat the same mistakes knowingly, the consequences escalate.

Take the example of my friend's grandmother. If I had confronted her and explained why her comment was harmful and she continued anyway, she would've been intentionally perpetuating harm, creating generational karma. The worst character flaw is pretending to be ignorant to avoid accountability. Ignorance may feel like bliss, but true joy comes from embracing truth with courage.

Our creator doesn't punish us; instead, we're guided to grow. Those who live closely with their higher consciousness often see their karma play out in shorter cycles. They recognize their missteps, correct them, and evolve. It's as if our creator is shaping us for greater understanding, like stones in a river being smoothed by the current.

Some lives, though short, teach us profound lessons. These earth angels remind us of innocence, purity, and the sacredness of life. They inspire us to reflect on our paths and strive for greater compassion.

Choosing ignorance is a betrayal of our higher self. Growth requires facing challenges, learning from mistakes, and acting with integrity. By doing so, we honor those who came before us and pave the way for those to follow, creating a heaven on earth.

Holding the Frequency

When you carry enlightenment, it comes with great responsibility. Who would've thought Buzz Lightyear would teach us so much? I mean, he had to be an astronaut hanging out with aliens to get it right? Okay, maybe not, but seriously—when you know better, there's no going back. There will be times, especially as you're breaking these old chains, that you'll feel like the black sheep. We touched on this in Code One, but this time, it's not just your family—it's your environment, your social circles, the digital spaces you exist in, and even your own mind when no one else is looking.

Tests will come, and they'll challenge you to see if you're truly carrying the light. That's the essence of holding a higher frequency. It's not a casual thing you can pick up and drop when it's convenient. It requires you to *hold* it.

Picture this: your partner comes home from work, cranky as hell, walking through the door with a laundry list of complaints about what's going wrong. Or maybe you're out to dinner with a friend who's throwing bratty energy all over the table. Or worse, you're at a restaurant, and the waiter gives you the most dismissive, horrible service. What's your reaction?

Naturally, the old you might want to match their energy—shut down, reserve yourself, or, on a really bad day, snap back and give them a piece of your mind. But now that you think you're not ignorant, now that you know better, *can you hold the frequency?* Are you actively raising vibrations in these moments, or are you letting the energy pull you down?

This isn't just about staying "calm" or "positive." It's about creating an opportunity to raise the frequency. When your partner walks in fuming, can you offer empathy and a calm presence that softens their mood? When your friend is spiraling into entitlement, can you lovingly guide the conversation somewhere lighter? And when the waiter is giving you horrible service, can you remember that they're likely dealing with their own battles, and leave them with kindness instead of resentment?

Holding the frequency goes beyond these interactions, too. It's in the music you listen to, the conversations you choose to have, the foods you eat, and the intentions you carry. All of these seemingly small choices affect not just your personal vibration but the collective experience.

When you consistently hold the frequency, you become the kind of energy that transforms a room the moment you walk in. You add value simply by existing. People don't just feel better around you—they become better.

So why does this matter? Because raising your vibration raises the collective consciousness. When you refuse to let low-frequency energy pull you down, you're showing others what's possible. You're proving that joy, love, and peace aren't just idealistic concepts—they're attainable. And the more of us that hold these higher frequencies, the more we shift the collective energy.

Think of it this way: every time you hold the frequency, you're planting seeds. Maybe that seed grows into someone else having a better day. Maybe it inspires them to carry that energy forward to someone else. And slowly, those seeds become a forest, raising consciousness for all of humanity.

But here's the real question: *Can you hold it when it's hard?* When the energy in the room is thick and heavy, when someone's testing your patience, when the world feels like it's spinning in chaos—can you still hold the light? Because that's where the real work happens.

And here's the truth: every time you do, you align yourself closer to your higher self. Every choice to raise the vibration is a step toward your soul's evolution. It's not easy—it's not meant to be. But it's worth it. Because when you hold the frequency, you're not just healing yourself; you're healing the collective. And that's the kind of legacy that changes the world.

The Equinox

Just like the rhythmic cycle of the Earth, life itself is all about balance—a dance between light and shadow. The equinox, where day and night hold equal sway, is a reminder from the universe to recognize that both our joys and our pains are powerful teachers. It's not about denying one or the other but finding harmony between the two. Our struggles, like our victories, are part of the journey. They're not obstacles to dodge but lanterns guiding us toward deeper self-discovery.

This time of balance reassures us that we're on a path we can trust, encouraging us to integrate our shadows and let them reveal insights that wouldn't surface in the light alone. In healing, it's not about mimicking what's trendy in wellness circles or trying to fit into someone else's mold. Your journey might not look like the crystal-infused, sea moss-eating influencer; it might look like morning heavy metal and evening Gucci Mane. Your darkness is subjective, personal, and uniquely yours to embrace—and loving yourself exactly as you are, in ways that no one else can understand, is called being authentic.

I get questions all the time about where to draw the line on spiritual practices, who to trust for an energy cleanse, or whether things like tarot or certain rituals cross into "too much." But here's the thing—spirituality isn't one-size-fits-all. Think of it like a baptism. Have you been to one recently? They're literally dunking a baby's head in water, and in some traditions, smudging them with incense. But at its core, it's a cleansing, a ritual of protection. All these practices, whether it's gentle healing or an intense exorcism, play vital roles in the spiritual ecosystem.

It's always interesting to hear religious leaders call these "occult" practices evil or say that psychics are conjuring demonic forces, especially considering that since the beginning of time, every ancient text and book of wisdom has pointed to prophets leading people through the darkest times.

I consider myself a lightworker, which means I stick to practices that resonate with the positives. I like to work with light and pull from there; I consider myself a master gift organizer. I can see someone, and within five minutes of speaking to them, I can tell what their divine gifts are and walk them through actionable steps on how to execute them, including what energetic blockages are in the way. I know my limits, and I respect those who dive deeper into the heavy lifting. For those navigating intense trauma or dark attachments, I might even recommend working with another type of practitioner, someone skilled in those specific areas. Plus, let's face it, society doesn't need another white girl calling herself a shaman. Each practice—whether dealing with the unseen, facilitating transitions to the afterlife, or lifting curses— requires a unique skill set. And yes, you'll see more of these healers and shamans now than ever before because we're in the middle of a cosmic shift. Humanity is waking up to the need for collective healing, which means the call for all kinds of spiritual workers has never been louder.

Whenever I sit with someone who feels that pull to become a healer, I take it seriously. That calling is there for a reason. Each person stepping into their role contributes to this collective wave of growth, healing, and unity. Like the equinox reminds us of balance in nature, this is our time to bring balance within ourselves, honoring both the light and the dark, and walking the path with self-love, respect, and unwavering integrity.

In doing this, we're creating the kind of world where spiritual practices are respected, where people aren't afraid to ask questions, and where growth, healing, and connection are at the center. Just like the equinox, it's a powerful, universal call to align, to heal, and to remember: embracing our light and darkness is our way forward, but understanding that light is the glory that saves us.

The wound is where light enters you, the cycle of life and death echoes the balance of the equinox, where neither day nor night reigns supreme. Just as the equinox marks transitions, life and death remind us of the continuity within the cosmos, where endings merge into **beginnings** in the Creator's warmth.

This cosmic rhythm inspires us to see rebirth in our daily lives, an opportunity to shed what no longer serves us and embrace renewal. Each day, we're given the chance to transform ourselves, to leave behind outdated beliefs, relationships, and habits. It's a process that might require us to part ways with familiar paths or companions that no longer align with our growth.

Embracing this cycle of personal rebirth, much like the natural world greets each new season, allows us to move forward with grace. It's a journey of continual transformation, where every moment of release opens the door to new beginnings and possibilities.

I once heard an interview where they asked Mike Tyson what he believed classified him as an inspiration to the world. Without hesitation, he responded by saying, "To die over and over again in front of millions of people." You see, when you are willing to be bare and raw in front of what seems like the world, there is nothing that you cannot achieve. The beauty of death is that although you may be alone, lose those you loved and those who you thought loved you, lose your lifestyle, there is still one thing that you come away with, and that is your wisdom. Your spirit recalls this, making you stronger in your next spiritual encounter.

The best is yet to come

The journey we are on is leading us toward a culmination of beauty, wisdom, and joy that is beyond our current comprehension. The target must be so massive that it is beyond you.

The point of it all, then, is to engage in this journey with our whole beings, to embrace each breath as an opportunity to move closer to that divine culmination. Where we stand now is to truly experience heaven on earth is to understand that there is an even greater place that exists and to enter it see that it is now. It's in understanding that our actions, thoughts, and intentions ripple through the universe, influencing not just our own paths but those of others, weaving us together. This perspective shifts our focus from the self to the collective, from the tangible to the transcendent, aligning our purposes with something far greater than ourselves. It suggests that our individual lives, while seemingly finite, are integral chapters in an endless story of spiritual evolution and enlightenment.

Imagine if we put forth into the world acted as seeds, growing into forests of bliss. Like the extra time we take to pick up clothes that fell off the rack while shopping or let that person on the road cut us off. What if, in moments of hurt and thoughts of retribution, we heard a whisper from the Creator, a reassurance that our pains are seen, and justice lies not in our hands but in the balance of the universe? This realization elevates the human experience from a struggle for survival and vindication to an opportunity not only to experience bliss but to spread bliss. That is code eight, realizing that it's not about you, it is about understanding that your actions and experiences play a key part in the collective consciousness.

Bliss, in its purest form, is devoid of the lower vibrations of revenge, division, and ego. It is a state of being that transcends the human-made boundaries and conflicts, offering a glimpse of heaven on earth. To live in bliss is to let go of the weights that tether our spirits to the mundane, to embrace a love and peace that flows freely, unobstructed by the scars of our journeys.

The legacy we leave behind, then, becomes a reflection of how closely we've aligned our lives with these higher principles.

We are the youngest participants in the cosmic order

The Miracle of Life

Even with the ability to be able to even take a deep breath in and sit here and read these very words we overlook the miracle of life itself. We are both the creators and the observers of our reality. It tells us of the delicate dance between matter and energy, the seen and the unseen, the tangible and the spiritual.

Embracing nature's rhythm, our world races at a speed, worshipping at the altar of instant gratification, yet the essence of true living breathes in the slow, deliberate rhythms of the earth. Deep down we know we should honor the natural cycle of things, where the value lies not in how quickly we accomplish our tasks, but in the depth and richness of our experiences. It encourages us to build communities that reflect this slower pace, fostering deep connections with each other and the world around us. You are lucky enough that you can walk and breathe and listen so closely.

We know this deep within because we carry a library within. Imagine our bodies as libraries, vast and filled with knowledge, where each cell holds stories, and every breath turns a page. Before our arrival in this form, our souls, acting as meticulous librarians, select the experiences we need, guided by a blueprint of past learnings. Life, then, is not a linear journey but a collection of moments existing simultaneously, urging us to see beyond the physical. We are not merely the beads of experiences on the string of existence; we are the string itself, constant and unchanging amidst the flux.

The Conscious Collective

When I first started organizing my retreats, I knew they would be powerful. I had zero doubts or hesitations—I knew these messages had to be delivered. With God on my side, I felt the privilege and responsibility of carefully curating the group of people attending these retreats. I decided early on that I wanted to hand-select each person who attended, intentionally sitting down to get to know everyone who showed interest. And even when no one initially showed interest, I performed a spiritual practice on social media, letting God channel me to the people who were in need of this experience. I knew my purpose was to align people with their highest mission.

Most of us are simply getting by, feeling alone or misguided— not because we lack vision or resources but because we haven't set aside the time to sit down and remember who we truly are and what we're capable of. For instance, you might say you want a million dollars, but the reality is, you wouldn't know what to do with even an extra ten thousand if it came your way. There's no alignment, no attraction, no chemistry; you're like a kid wanting shiny things but with no real connection to them. Or maybe you say you want an incredible partner to love, someone to share dates with and build a family alongside, but you haven't yet learned to embrace your own presence or even take yourself out on a date.

Or perhaps you're longing for a new circle of friends—ones who are ambitious, soulful, and driven. But you haven't spent a single minute listening to a podcast, attending an event, or investing in yourself in ways that would align you with these types of people. Here's the truth: the things you want in life want you even more, but those things require true alignment. That's the real manifestation.

Over my 15 years of training, I developed a deep activation exercise I call the "Million Dollar Question." It's a magical prompt that started as a hypnosis meditation. This exercise has worked for me and 99% of my students, helping us uncover the reasons we were sent here to this planet. And yes, I leave one key piece out—because, let's face it, some people say they want to awaken but don't actually want to face the change it demands.

One of the biggest revelations people have during this activation is that their purpose isn't just about themselves. There's something much bigger than us, and that's why their role hasn't yet been fulfilled. The entire time, we've been focusing on showing up for ourselves, not realizing that we're here on this planet to be beams of everlasting, unconditional love. As cheesy as it might sound, we often don't have the courage to show up for ourselves the way we'd show up for others.

It's in moments of despair—like when someone reaches that point where they're questioning if they should even be here—that the understanding clicks. They feel the weight of their purpose, their importance, and the undeniable truth that they're deeply connected to the lives around them. I call this the ripple effect.

We're all interconnected, just like a family of trees. When one tree is cut off, the neighboring trees send resources to help it survive. The same goes for the hidden network in the mushroom family, a system that supports and nourishes each other beneath the surface. This is community in its most natural, sacred form.

During these retreats, I realized one of the biggest takeaways was that sometimes, having a friend to vent to, a parent to call and pour your heart out to, a therapist to listen and give advice, or a coach to hold you accountable—none of these alone may be enough to truly heal. Sometimes, what we actually need is a combination of all these roles around us in a circle—a community of people who may look like strangers at first but, in that moment, hold the power to witness, hear, and support you. A group where you can scream it out, be seen, be heard, and be held by a community.

This is the embodiment of Christ consciousness. This is the power behind religions, churches, cults—call it whatever you will—but at the core, it's a craving that humans have without needing labels. It's about sitting with people from all walks of life, welcoming a stranger, and discovering a shared path that's been walked before. This is the Conscious Collective.

If any part of this resonates with you, if you feel called to explore these activations, reach out. My team and I are here, and we invite you to join us on this journey. Email us to receive the activation meditation for free at info@houseofvibration.com and step into this powerful space of growth and alignment together.

Dripped in Codes

Humans are often seen as the final brushstroke, the youngest participants in the cosmic order. This youthfulness is not a mark of naivety but a sign of our potential to continually contribute to the universal compendium of knowledge. Like the serpent that sheds its skin, we are microcosms of the universe, learning and evolving, our DNA a double helix that encodes the mysteries of the cosmos. Within us lies not a linear path but a spiral, embodying the essence of existence—cyclical, ever-changing, and boundless. There's beauty in this spiral, no incorrect perspective, only a journey of rises and falls, always moving forward.

Close your eyes and take a deep, slow breath, drawing in the sacred energy of the cosmos. As you inhale, imagine a radiant, shimmering light entering through the crown of your head, flowing down your spine like a warm, luminous river. Feel this divine light filling you with peace, vitality, and spiritual nourishment. As you exhale, envision this light spiralling outwards, expanding into the infinite expanse of the universe. With each breath, see the air as a double helix of golden strands, intertwining and connecting you to the stars, while feeling the grounding embrace of Pachamama, Mother Earth, rising up to nourish your spirit.

Imagine yourself in a cosmic dance, where humans are the final brushstroke in the grand order of existence. This sacred youthfulness signifies our potential to contribute to the universal compendium of wisdom. Envision a serpent transforming, symbolizing your own spiritual evolution. Your essence holds the divine mysteries of life. Within you lies a spiral path, embodying the cyclical, ever-changing, and boundless nature of existence. Picture this spiral as a glowing path through your life, connecting past, present, and future. Now, imagine God gently placing the

166

sacred eighth code atop your crown, infusing you with divine wisdom and light. Embrace this sacred flow, feeling the harmony of the cosmos within you, and know that with each breath, you are both a student and a teacher, part of an eternal dance of creation and spiritual growth. You are now Bliss Coded.

By committing to embracing the full spectrum of life, ensuring that your legacy is not one of sorrow but a testament to love and vibrancy. In acknowledging the spiral of our being and the universe, we understand that every lesson, every strand of DNA, offers insights into the celestial realm itself. Our existence is a reflection of the universe—complex, interconnected, and infinitely expanding. Embrace this journey with an open heart.

Final Activation for Code Eight: Infinite Purpose & The Conscious Collective

As you complete this journey, Code Eight brings you to the heart of your mission—the reason you came here, the pulse of the collective soul that beats within each of us. You've walked the path, peeling back layers, meeting your fears, unlocking codes within you that align with something far greater than the self. Now, you stand ready to embody your highest purpose, woven into the conscious web of humanity, grounded in the wisdom of all directions—north, south, east, and west. You are both the healer and the healed, the seeker and the guide, the individual and the infinite. The universe watches with open arms, ready for the gifts you now carry forward.

This final code asks you to stand tall, to know that everything you've learned here is a thread in the tapestry of all you will leave behind. You are part of something boundless and ancient—a lineage of souls who have chosen love, unity, and awakening. There is no destination; this mission is ongoing, an infinite expansion of light that you now carry in each step, word, and breath.

Reflective Questions:

Now that you've been heard, felt, and understood, ask yourself: Will I hold steady alongside my brothers and sisters on this sacred mission, the one my highest self sent me here to fulfill? Close your eyes, envisioning your life's highest purpose unfolding in each moment. Allow your third eye to show you the life waiting for you—a life connected, aligned, and courageous. Ask yourself, Will I allow my mission to guide me beyond fear, beyond illusions, into the eternal flow of creation?

If you feel called to go deeper, if this final activation stirs something within you, send your reflections to **info@houseofvibration.com.** In return, you'll receive the final activation meditation—a guided journey to root this purpose in every layer of your being, so that your light may radiate through every moment of your life.

Affirmations for Code Eight:

- I am the living legacy of all that came before and all that will follow, connected to the conscious web of humanity.

- I trust in my purpose, knowing I am here to uplift, heal, and expand in alignment with all.

- My mission transcends fear and limitation, opening pathways for growth, love, and unity.

- I honor the infinite within me, dedicating my life to the collective mission that guides us all home.

May your journey through these codes guide you to live fully, love deeply, and lead with the radiant truth of your highest self. This is not an end but the beginning of a new chapter. Congratulations on embracing the sacred, stepping fully into the mission you were born to live in true bliss.

Congrats you broke the cycle

Thank You to My Teachers

Viviane Perez

Jorge Enrique Restrepo

Jorge Hernan Restrepo

Jonathan Heinsohn

Hena Aleman

Carolina Gonzalez

Gustavo Fallas

Luz Helena Restrepo

Bear Heart

Paramahansa

Lynne Twist

Maru Chavez

Grant Cardone

Luz Duque

Mahina Alexander

Lisa Campion

Carmen Febrero